JOURNEY BACK TO MY INDIGENOUS ROOTS

Conquering Paper Genocide

By

Chief Zakiya Hahta Nashoba

© Copyright (2019) by

(Chief Zakiya Hahta Nashoba) - All rights reserved.

It is not legal to reproduce, duplicate, or transmit any part of this document in either electronic means or printed format.

Recording of this publication is strictly prohibited.

ISBN 978-0-578-47192-1

I dedicate this book to

My bloodline

My Parents (Linda and James)

My Daughters (Shi'ra and Niah)

I dedicate this book to everyone who is conquering Paper Genocide by restoring their Indigenous Identity.

Special thanks to

Ronald Carter Skyhand (Chahta)

My Cousin Jameel Shamsid-Deen (Lumbee)

My cousin Jzoe (Arawak)

My cousin Amber King (Cherokee)

Honorable mention to everyone actively telling their story.

Table of Contents

Introduction 1

PART I: My Childhood   2

    Chapter One: Living in the Black Power Era 14

    Chapter Two: New Beginning................................26

PART II: My Journey 44

    Chapter Three: My Travels.....................................58

    Chapter Four: Urban Myths 101

    Chapter Five: Not Good Enough 113

Acknowledgments 172

About the Author 174

Disclaimer:

This book may challenge your belief system.

This book may cause you to feel anger, joy or doubt.

This book may challenge everything you have been taught.

This book may cause you to dig deeper into your own roots.

This book may make you see past previous social conditioning.

This book may not fulfill your expectations.

The names mentioned to identify indigenous peoples in this book are all colonized terms and is not ancient.

Cherokee, Choctaw, Mayan etc. are not what the ancients called themselves these are modern terms, I use them for the sake of familiarity however I acknowledge that my ancient ancestors did not utilize these terms prior to Christian European invasion.

The term European used throughout the book is referring to Europe it is not referring to any particular skin tone ancient Europe was all dark skin people and a lot of their descendants played/plays an active role in colonizing.

This book is my story based upon my research into my family roots and into the origins of the first peoples of what we now call America (Continent), it is not my complete story, however it gives the reader a glimpse into my journey.

I wrote this book while battling Vitamin D deficiency please have your levels tested because what I am feeling I wouldn't wish on my worst enemy.

I am one out of millions who have suffered paper genocide, I am just one drop in the ocean of colonization.

I am just one out of millions who are decolonizing and reclaiming their indigenous heritage.

Any articles, pictures or quoted literature that is not owned by me is used under the fair use act for the purpose of teaching, where possible I will give reference to the source.

This page is dedicated to my totem

    The White Wolf is my guide and the Black Wolf is my protector on my journey.

    Both of them appeared to me in a vision

    The White Wolf showed up first as I was seeking truth and pulling away from the colonizers religion (Christianity).

The Black Wolf showed up a year later as my protector on this journey, one of my clans is Wolf Clan.

Introduction

Thank You for allowing me to tell my story

I have been researching exactly what happened to my family and how our Indigenous Identity was stolen from us.

I have utilized DNA and Genealogy to piece together my family's rich Indigenous American (continental) history.

I hope by me telling my story more indigenous people will research their family's heritage and step forward and let the world know that we are still here WE ARE NOT EXTINCT.

To my relations on the various Islands of the Americas just know that you are not alone we know who you are here on the mainland.

A JOURNEY BACK TO MY INDIGENOUS ROOTS BY ZAKIYA HAHTA NASHOBA

PART I: My Childhood

July 27th, 1973 in a local hospital in Ohio a baby girl was born to Linda and James at approximately 6:43 am

Unknown to Linda and James was the role I would play in restoring our family's indigenous American Identity.

My mother told me she had a normal pregnancy

When I was born my parents decided to wait three months until I came into my looks and personality to name me, they decided to name me Zakiya.

Zakiya means intelligent and pure in Arabic

Sakiya is the Aniyunwiya pronunciation

I have lived up to this name every since they named me

My Paternal Grandmother wanted to name me Mary after her but my mother said she is not a Mary.

A JOURNEY BACK TO MY INDIGENOUS ROOTS BY ZAKIYA HAHTA NASHOBA

Growing up I was the only girl among two boys so I learned to have a lot of me time, sometimes I would play football with my brothers and uncle, my mother didn't like me playing with them because they showed me no mercy, I remember a time when I got tackled so hard the wind was knocked out of me I couldn't breathe for a few seconds I was wheezing a lot, you would think I would have stopped playing but I went right back to playing I guess I was just hard headed plus I loved playing football.

Looking back, I can see that some of the best times was in my childhood.

I was never a follower being born as a Leo ruled by the Sun there was always a fire deep within me.

Even as a child I would speak for the ones who couldn't speak for themselves.

I can recall a time when I was about nine years old, we were in a hotel and it was absolutely horrible my mother called the manager to complain and he started trying to finesse my mother with excuses, I immediately jumped in with questions etc. he looked at me and said what are you some child lawyer?

A JOURNEY BACK TO MY INDIGENOUS ROOTS BY ZAKIYA HAHTA NASHOBA

Growing up everybody just knew I would be working as a lawyer I was on that path until I learned that the laws are all foreign to my people and quite frankly has done nothing but damage us.

Now my focus is on indigenous law not Federal laws.

I remember growing up in Ohio we would forage for wild chives, pawpaw, walnuts, chamomile, poke salat, crab apples, and whatever herbs that grew wild, my mother could identify most of them.

I remember we would forage wild Chamomile, Dandelion and Chives, we would make Chamomile Tea, my mother would fry the Dandelions and make potato and chive patties and fry it.

When times got hard, we would get that Gov't box full of fake cheese, honey, flour, cornmeal, powdered milk (this gave us horrible gas) Peanut butter, Beans, butter etc. my mother would work miracles with that box she made Pizza, burritos, cakes, cornmeal mush, biscuits, peanut butter cookies etc. all from that box.

My father was a hunter and fisher, he would hunt deer, rabbit and catch fish and bring it home for my mother to cook, I remember the first time I saw the rabbit being skinned and baked

I refused to eat it, I just couldn't get that cute bunny look out of my head.

A JOURNEY BACK TO MY INDIGENOUS ROOTS BY ZAKIYA HAHTA NASHOBA

Growing up my dad was so much of a country boy that fishing, hiking, crawdaddy catching, and swimming in the natural hot springs was considered a normal thing for us.

(We call it crawdaddy some people in other areas call them crawfish).

I remember wanting to go to amusement parks as a child I can recall one time he took us to a place that was called fantasy farm and a place called Americana, he doesn't care too much for crowded places neither do I that's why fishing and hiking was our go to activity.

I remember my brothers and I would be in the backseat of the car soaking wet from crawdaddy fishing in the creek, we would be fussing with each other, I would be complaining about how they kept putting their wet leg on me, my brothers loved to aggravate me because I was the only girl.

I remember as a teen on Saturday mornings we would watch cartoons, we only had one TV so we had to take a vote about what we would watch, I was out voted every single time because my brothers didn't want to watch "girly" cartoons so He-man, Thunder cats, Transformers etc. is what I had to watch I actually started liking the shows.

Once my mother made them let me watch something and they had to watch it with me I chose solid gold, I wanted to be a solid gold dancer so bad, my brothers hated that show.

A JOURNEY BACK TO MY INDIGENOUS ROOTS BY ZAKIYA HAHTA NASHOBA

My childhood saw some good times and it saw some bad times despite the bad times I am still standing strong, Colonization splintered my family into so many pieces that I am still trying to piece us back together, my family is still struggling with the effects of Colonization.

I can recall as a child nobody talked much about my Great Grandparents, I don't know why, they just never made it a point to tell us children, I think by the time I was born my family had already been fractured due to colonization.

Nobody seemed to want to talk about the past, the closest we got to talking about the past was when a recipe or remedy was being passed down because they would tell you who gave it to them.

Something happened that silenced my family, the more I research my family history the more I understand the silence,

it's hard for some family members to talk about the atrocities

my family thought they were protecting the next generation by not talking about who we are and what we endured.

When I was a child my mother cooked everything from scratch, she would cook poke salat, Collard greens, Salmon patties, macaroni and cheese, banana bread, hot water cornbread, drop biscuits, succotash, oatmeal cake with brown sugar icing etc.

I found out as an adult a lot of these are all indigenous American dishes.

We always had plants in the house, aloe vera plants was a staple in our home we used it for scrapes, cuts, and burns.

A JOURNEY BACK TO MY INDIGENOUS ROOTS BY ZAKIYA HAHTA NASHOBA

We would hang herbs on the porch to dry out and during the winter we would use the back porch as a fridge, we would get our milk from the farm non-pasteurized, we ate honeycombs, ginseng, honey suckle etc. and we rarely got sick at all.

When we had a cold, my father would give us a little shot of whiskey and make us sit in the sun so we could sweat it out and heal using the Sun rays.

I remember once when I was sick my father went in the kitchen and whipped up some type of home remedy, I thought he was being cheap at the time because he didn't go to the drugstore, now I know he was doing what indigenous people do.

Every rising my mother would give us a spoonful of be pollen, honey and cod liver oil.

My childhood was truly lived just being one with nature, it was during a time where we could drink from the natural springs that flowed through the park, we would hike in.

We either grew our food or went to the local farms to get our food, I don't recall going to grocery stores every week as we do now.

Looking back, we kept a lot of our indigenous ways

I can recall my mother telling me about wolves walking upright outside our home, some people call them skinwalkers.

Growing up my mother was into to astrology, numerology and understanding energy on a metaphysical level.

A JOURNEY BACK TO MY INDIGENOUS ROOTS BY ZAKIYA HAHTA NASHOBA

She is a Christian now but thankfully she retained some of her old ways, every now and then she will break free from the spell of Christianity and it's demonizing of indigenous ways.

I can remember growing up and hearing our customs labeled as superstitious like when we would never throw our hair away after cutting it and how we were told to never let people play in your hair because everyone shouldn't be touching your hair, also how we would not want anyone to sweep our feet with a broom, also the elders didn't like taking pictures they said it would capture your soul.

There is a custom that says when a woman is pregnant the person who aggravates her the most would mark the baby meaning the baby would have a birthmark or characteristics like them.

My youngest brother Jamar aggravated me so much when I was pregnant with my first child that now she has a birthmark under her lip in the exact place as his.

R.I.P Jamar (Youngest brother)

R.I.P James (Oldest brother)

I remember the elder women in the family would look at a child and tell which one of our ancestors had come back, they would say things like lawd this baby act just like Catherine she done came back in this child.

A JOURNEY BACK TO MY INDIGENOUS ROOTS BY ZAKIYA HAHTA NASHOBA

The elders could also tell when a woman was pregnant, the elder would dream of fish and could see that the woman's aura had changed and become brighter.

They also saw death before it came.

I remember before you wanted to get married you had to bring your spouse in front of the women and let them read him or her, they would instantly know if this person was right or wrong for you, we used to listen but now we just ignore these warnings.

My mother is very powerful she told me that I would be having girls and she also told me not to marry my husband, I didn't listen and married him anyway let's just say I should have listened to my mother because that marriage was hell on earth thank goodness it ended.

I will save the details for another book.

As a child I can recall seeing certain things that I could not explain like shadows moving around, once my mother was in the kitchen cooking downstairs and I was sitting on the landing downstairs leading to the upstairs, I looked upstairs and I saw my mother walk pass at the top of the stairs, there was no way she could walk up there because she had to come pass me to do so, I still don't know how she did that or what I saw.

I remember my father told me about a house he moved into once I was grown, he said there was a young spirit in the house that kept messing with his change and hiding his indigenous herb (weed) the young spirit seem to enjoy pulling pranks on my

A JOURNEY BACK TO MY INDIGENOUS ROOTS BY ZAKIYA HAHTA NASHOBA

father needless to say my father got tired of his games and eventually moved out the home.

Being from the South my family was deeply Christianized (Colonized) when I would ask questions about what I saw they would say it's evil, if I kept pushing the issue, they would get out that bottle of olive oil and slap some on my forehead and start praying for me.

My Father is a Buddhist and a practitioner of "magic" so when I would ask him, he would just try to steer me away from what came naturally out of fear I would venture into the wrong side of "magic" (manipulating people's energy for harm not good)

He kept saying you are not ready, to this day he hasn't told me his full story.

Once I became an adult, I realized a lot of people have certain gifts that are passed down to them, however because of religion they are shunned or demonized, my daddy told me that his father was called a water witch because he could get a stick and find exactly where to build a well using only that stick and his energy.

There was once a time these gifts would be celebrated and utilized for the betterment of the community now, they are condemned.

Although I experienced so much good as a child, I had some not so good times.

The worst time in my childhood is when my brother's and I was kidnapped by the European system called child welfare,

A JOURNEY BACK TO MY INDIGENOUS ROOTS BY ZAKIYA HAHTA NASHOBA

I was 10 years old, my oldest brother was 11, and my youngest was 9 years old we were taken from my mother, they labeled her and my father witches.

They called my mother crazy because she spoke of her indigenous beliefs.

I was held in captivity for two years and placed in a foster home all by myself, they separated me from my brother's this is one of the reason's I don't depend on anyone for anything (at my own detriment), I had to depend on myself at the tender age of 10 this affects my ability to fully trust anyone (I am actively working on this soul wound) as I write this many indigenous children are in the system battling for their lives and so many have been harmed at the hand of strangers, thank goodness I never endured such harm, many children don't make it out alive.

If you have a family member who is struggling with parenting DO NOT allow your bloodline to be placed in the custody of strangers fight for them.

My experience in the system led me to become a foster parent and a Guardian ad Litem (child advocate).

Talking to the storm.

Once upon a time we use to communicate to the storm so that it would not harm us.

Here in Florida when the hurricane was coming, I talked to the storm and burned sage outside my home, my street didn't receive any flooding or major damage however the streets in front of me and behind me did.

A JOURNEY BACK TO MY INDIGENOUS ROOTS BY ZAKIYA HAHTA NASHOBA

The hurricane before that was in Texas I didn't speak to the storm and my street was flooded just from the heavy rain fall.

I speak to my environment daily I have learned to appreciate everything in my environment to include the fire ants that stay biting up my feet because I love to walk barefooted, I can't help it I have been barefooted since birth and I can't stand to have closed shoes on all day, I can tolerate flip flops because they let my feet breathe.

The older I get the simpler I want to live.

A JOURNEY BACK TO MY INDIGENOUS ROOTS BY ZAKIYA HAHTA NASHOBA

A JOURNEY BACK TO MY INDIGENOUS ROOTS BY ZAKIYA HAHTA NASHOBA

Chapter One: Living in The Black Power Era

I was born long after my people called themselves by their indigenous names and my great grandparents were labeled colored folk by European Immigrants.

I was born during a time of "Black power" and "Black pride".

I was born during a time that people with dark to light brown skin were called black, later own these same people were called African American without even having a choice about what they wanted to be called, somehow having any degree of brown skin lumps you into a generic category which involves multiple political designations (name changes) at the whim of whomever.

I was born during a time where if you did not identify with being black you had nowhere to go because the white folk didn't want you and the black folk didn't trust you, after all by that time people had been reduced down to skin color and hair texture.

I remember as a teenager I would say why is it always about black people and white people yet I see so many different people walking around do they not exist?

A JOURNEY BACK TO MY INDIGENOUS ROOTS BY ZAKIYA HAHTA NASHOBA

I must note that the term White and Black is strictly a political form of a class system (have and have not's) none of those terms define a person's true bloodline.

Speaking about the term African American I remember when I first heard that term, I instantly said what the hell is this?

Somehow Jesse Jackson and his handlers decided that millions of people would be defined as two continents, In later years I met Jesse Jackson at the National Black Caucas conference in Washington DC (2017) I was in my Tribal wear people couldn't figure out why an Indian would be there, I had many people approach me and share their own stories of there Indian heritage and some asked me how did I find out about my heritage?.

Let that phrase soak in "Find out"

I recall the Capitol police was interested in why I was there, I told them relax I will be leaving in the am, back to Jesse Jackson while I was there, he just kept staring at me as if remembering his own indigenous roots.

Jesse Jackson paternal line surname is Robinson he shares one of my Paternal surnames Robinson is common among the Cherokee.

A JOURNEY BACK TO MY INDIGENOUS ROOTS BY ZAKIYA HAHTA NASHOBA

Everywhere I looked I saw people beaming with pride of being "black" yet they had no clear definition of blackness, someone who looks nearly white would be called black because they had thick lips and curly hair or they would make people an honorary black if you acted like you liked them, you would be labeled black simply because you played the part or looked the part of this undefined blackness and if you rejected that label look out for insults and threats of bodily harm etc.

I recall learning about Martin Luther King Jr during black history month by the way he also has American Indian roots however he is always labeled as a black man.

I quickly learned that there is an old system that has been in existence beginning with the Vatican and that system is to destroy indigenous peoples globally to include the global amnesia of true historical events and the true heirs of the soil.

The system of teaching the children of your enemy among other systems aka Public-school system, aka Indian school system, aka kill the Indian save the man.

A JOURNEY BACK TO MY INDIGENOUS ROOTS BY ZAKIYA HAHTA NASHOBA

When I was much younger, I couldn't understand why in school we only learned about the accomplishments of "Black" people one month out of the year and it wasn't even a complete picture of the accomplishments.

I now know it was a systematic psychological programming to implant the feeling of being less then, this is implanted into the impressionable mind of a child making them ripe for future abuses that they would experience at the hands of European immigrants all in the name of false superiority.

Outside of black history month there was NO variety offered in the public-school systems (prison camp).

Wearing your hair in any style that did not require you to restrain your curls was seen as defiant, individuality and intellectual thought was met with severe punishment to include paddling, detention aka imprisonment and nowadays children are catching felonies in these school systems.

Showing any sort of individuality was deemed as a threat to the good of the school community (sounds like an occult).

A JOURNEY BACK TO MY INDIGENOUS ROOTS BY ZAKIYA HAHTA NASHOBA

I remember I had this European teacher, in our class we had this red head kid named Shane (I think he was Irish) he loved to play pranks, one day he decided to hide in the lockers that was in our classroom, the teacher found out and locked him in the lockers the entire classroom she placed scissors where the lock go so he couldn't get out, we were told to ignore his cries I was terrified I recall seeing another teacher walk into the classroom she heard Shane's cries but ignored it at that moment I realized I was surrounded by some of the most deviant people in our society, as soon as I got home I told my mother, the next morning she was at school cussing them out and had me removed from that classroom.

(she should have removed me from that entire school system)

I could tell you some horror stories of what these European's did to children in their schools.

I recall the days of paddling my mother wasn't having any of that thank goodness she was not the type of parent that believed any and everything strangers (teachers) told her about her child, once a teacher wanted to paddle me because I would not allow this student to take my crayons and bully me.

A JOURNEY BACK TO MY INDIGENOUS ROOTS BY ZAKIYA HAHTA NASHOBA

My school years were traumatizing and full of forced assimilation.

There was absolutely nothing in the curriculum that spoke of indigenous peoples in a positive way, the education was centered on Europeans and their conquest.

I remember my mother told me as a teenager she got suspended from school all because she wore an afro, she told me that they thought she was militant, my mother is a Leo like me so I am sure she was just as defiant as me and was questioning everything.

To be honest I was forced fed "Blackness" by the school system, media and my brainwashed peers.

In the United Colonies (U.S.A) nothing exists outside of a Black and white paradigm, during the time of my childhood we had no internet that allowed us to see beyond the deception of the colony's political paradigm of black and white.

A JOURNEY BACK TO MY INDIGENOUS ROOTS BY ZAKIYA HAHTA NASHOBA

I learned very quickly that in the United Colonies aka United States if you are presumed to be of any degree of Negro (Portuguese word for black aka dark in color) you are "Black" it doesn't matter what your Tribal or National affiliation is you were instantly placed into a lower class designation which came with a target on your back, not much has changed this is still the case in 2019 if you are of American descendant.

A JOURNEY BACK TO MY INDIGENOUS ROOTS BY ZAKIYA HAHTA NASHOBA

Dashikis and Ankhs

My pan African Sisters and Brothers aka mislabeled and Misguided indigenous people.

As a young adult I found it really easy to sit with people and talk about "black" issues and "black" struggles after all I shared the same struggle and issues plus, we all had been lumped into the pot black because our skin was not deficient in Melanin because we retained the color of our ancient pre-Colombian ancestors.

I didn't see any other group of people that would collectively talk about the issues that affected me, we never really talked about our heritage outside of knowing we all had American Indian blood in our family but we pushed that to the side and focused on "black" issues it wasn't until later in life that I realized black was just a descriptive term and had nothing to do with Nationality or Ancestral lineage.

Growing up so many people knew of their American Indian ancestry that it became an urban myth.

A JOURNEY BACK TO MY INDIGENOUS ROOTS BY ZAKIYA HAHTA NASHOBA

I am sure you have heard this question

Why black people always say they got Indian in them?

Seems like they say this because it is the truth and they believe what their elders have told them.

Many studies have been done confirming that so-called African Americans have Indigenous American ancestry yet somehow the social political term of black and African American have been forced upon the people removing them from their own bloodline.

Some of our "Black" leaders and musicians have American Indian ancestry but media seems to focus more on their skin color versus their bloodline.

I can recall asking some of the most Pro Black people I knew about their Indigenous American heritage, they would beam with pride as they say my grandma/great grandma is full blood Cherokee etc.

I don't recall anyone saying anything less than full blood.

Then they would begin to talk about their grandmothers and describe how they would cook certain foods and their home remedies.

A JOURNEY BACK TO MY INDIGENOUS ROOTS BY ZAKIYA HAHTA NASHOBA

I remember we would all talk about how our mothers would cook Salmon patties, Poke salat, Collard greens, Turnip Greens, Sun tea etc.

If you couldn't throw down in the kitchen you would be questioned as to why? because cooking was a loving activity, our grandmothers would cook out of love especially picking the right healing herbs, meats etc. to keep our family healthy and strong,

Love is the most important ingredient in our food and we can taste when it's not there.

Our women have a thing where they refuse to cook anything mad, if they are mad at you, they will not cook anything for you, cooking is truly an activity of love.

Food is for the healing of the soul, we use to honor our parents, grandparents and the food for nourishing our bodies but after colonization we started thanking Jesus instead.

Although they knew of their Indian heritage it was black power that they clung to.

The Pro black era was a movement of empowering people of color but it came with certain strict beliefs one of the most damaging

A JOURNEY BACK TO MY INDIGENOUS ROOTS BY ZAKIYA HAHTA NASHOBA

beliefs is that ALL so- called African Americans are descendants of slaves that came from Africa (Tribes unknown) and that there is no way to find out where your people come from.

These beliefs systems are based upon emotions and not actual facts.

The Pro Black era was a time of a lot of social pressure if you didn't identify with being "black" you were told that you were ashamed of who you are, somehow you became an enemy just because you didn't identify with being black, simply because you identified with what your parents and grandparents taught you.

Even today this same bully tactic is utilized among

Some Pro Black supporters everyone wants to Africanize you because it makes them feel good.

No wonder why so many people just stay quiet about their indigenous heritage, they are afraid of being bullied and brutalized.

A JOURNEY BACK TO MY INDIGENOUS ROOTS BY ZAKIYA HAHTA NASHOBA

I have endured my own verbal attacks by saying I am American Indian, some pro-black people would do all they can to try and make me African from trying to make me seem like I am a trader, I am ashamed to be "black" etc.

I also received racial epithets from some Native Americans saying that I am African and a slave these words normally come from people who believe the racist rhetoric taught to them by their elders, they seem to have somehow forgotten that we are the ancient of the ancients, I blame the elders that sided with the European immigrants and decided to practice racism which happens to run rampant in Indian country it's one of those taboo subjects they **REFUSE** to address.

A JOURNEY BACK TO MY INDIGENOUS ROOTS BY ZAKIYA HAHTA NASHOBA

Chapter Two: New Beginning

I was still living in Ohio when I started having a strong pulling to move to Florida, I felt like I just couldn't breathe anymore in Ohio.

I had a strong desire to move further south so I started making plans to make the move.

I was 33 when I moved to Florida with my 10-year-old daughter and my 3-month-old daughter.

Writing this right now I noticed the spiritual meaning behind my move at that particular time.

I will do the numerology breakdown.

33 (my age)

10 (my daughter age)

3 months (my youngest daughter age)

33+10+3=46 this has to be broken down

4+6=10 break this down 1+0=1

1 is the number of new beginnings

A JOURNEY BACK TO MY INDIGENOUS ROOTS BY ZAKIYA HAHTA NASHOBA

Guided by my ancestors

I was new to Florida but I was very comfortable I felt like I had returned home.

In Florida I was surrounded by so much diversity, I noticed people celebrated their Nationality and Tribal affiliation it was nothing like where I grew up in Ohio where only colors existed i.e. Black and White.

While in Florida I worked at many Jobs to include being a corrections officer in a maximum-security prison, that job was hard on my soul I saw too many of my people incarcerated, the youngest person there was a 16-year-old child being kept in inhumane conditions I couldn't be a participant in that type of treatment to my people so I quit.

I left that job and went to work for the Seminole Tribe of Florida as a security officer at the Casino on the Big Cypress Reservation.

While I was working there, I had an incident with two non-Tribal employees, I was at work one night when they said to each other we can't make our jokes anymore as they looked at me,

A JOURNEY BACK TO MY INDIGENOUS ROOTS BY ZAKIYA HAHTA NASHOBA

I looked at them and said if it has nothing to do with race why wouldn't you?

I decided to talk to my boss about the incident, I told him what happened, he was upset over what happened and insisted I make a report so I did.

The Tribe handled the investigation very well.

This was my first encounter with a Florida Cracker the gentleman who was a participant in saying he couldn't say his jokes anymore called himself this proudly, I was new to Florida so I was unfamiliar with that term although when I worked at the Prison the term cracker was used often among the inmates.

My boss name was Tiger he is Seminole some people would ignorantly call him a Black Seminole instead of by his Nationality and that's simply Seminole, there is no need to insert a color, anyway I would talk to Tiger about his heritage and it intrigued me, see at the time I didn't know about my Seminole Heritage yet my ancestors placed me there to spark curiosity in me.

A JOURNEY BACK TO MY INDIGENOUS ROOTS BY ZAKIYA HAHTA NASHOBA

Tiger was a badass he didn't take shit from no one he would show up to work riding on his Harley racing down the road, truth be told if I would have saw him outside of the Reservation, he would have looked no different then your average so called black male.

Tiger sparked the fire deep within to want to know more about who I am.

When I stopped working for the Tribe, I was on a journey of wanting to know more.

In Florida, it's normal for people to ask where do you come from?

I got asked all the time what are you?

I remember going in the store one time when my youngest daughter was 5 months old, the store owner swore up and down my youngest daughter was Puerto Rican I told him no she isn't.

I didn't know at that time that I actually do have grandparents from there (Taino).

A JOURNEY BACK TO MY INDIGENOUS ROOTS BY ZAKIYA HAHTA NASHOBA

I got tired of all the what are you? questions so I decided I am too old not to know exactly where I come from, I have children and they deserve to know so I decided to take a DNA test.

I researched for months about the company that would be best for me, I decided not to go with the more popular companies.

I ordered the test in 2016 and waited the two weeks it takes to get the results.

Two weeks had passed and I finally received an email saying your results are in I don't know why I was nervous but I was.

I opened the email and I was instantly confused I saw all of these results saying I matched people in Virginia, Tennessee, Kentucky, Mississippi, Puerto Rico, Ecuador, Jamaica, Brazil etc. (I didn't know how valuable this would be but once I did my genealogy I quickly found out)

Then I saw that I was American Indian from Florida with two Alleles I called the Doctor I needed him to explain the two alleles to me, the Doctor told me usually in autosomal testing you don't know which parent you inherited the gene from however in your

A JOURNEY BACK TO MY INDIGENOUS ROOTS BY ZAKIYA HAHTA NASHOBA

case since both of your parents are American Indian it shows as two alleles and because of this you are American Indian more than anything else.

This certificate has my Tribal name and my Christianized surname, I omitted my family surname for privacy.

DNA Consultants

THIS DOCUMENT CERTIFIES THAT

Zakiya H▬▬▬▬▬

Zakiya Hahta Nashoba

Ordered a Native American DNA Fingerprint Plus from Our Laboratories
Yielding the Following American Indian Matches

Native American - Florida (n = 105)
Native American II marker (two alleles)
Megapopulations - American Indian Rank # 10

Donald N. Yates
Principal Investigator, DNA Consultants, P.O. Box 2477, Longmont, CO 80502

August 23, 2016

American Indian Index: 3.28E+12 (Very Common)
This number expresses how common or rare your DNA profile is in 24 American Indian populations. A figure such as 7.12E+16 means you have a 1 in 71200000000000000 random match probability, or 1 in 71 quadrillion. The range is 10 (very common) to 22 (extremely rare). Compared to your overall world index of 7.22E+12, your American Indian index shows you are more likely to be American Indian than anything else.

A JOURNEY BACK TO MY INDIGENOUS ROOTS BY ZAKIYA HAHTA NASHOBA

After that phone call I was shocked because in school all I had been taught was dark skin people meant Africa and slavery, I started breaking my DNA down more and I realized if I match all these so-called African Americans and I was American Indian that means they are to.

THE FIRE WAS FULLY IGNITED

I had to find out what happened that my family got renamed Colored, Mullato, Black, White, Negro and now African American.

At this point, the burning question in most people head is do you have any African ancestry? to that, I say no because Africa is a Continent, not a people.

I haven't found any genealogical records saying that any of my grandparents came from Africa via a slave trade or otherwise and my family hasn't passed down any home remedies or recipes from the continent of Africa, if I find any grandparents that came from the Continent, I will embrace them just like I embraced my European grandparents.

A JOURNEY BACK TO MY INDIGENOUS ROOTS BY ZAKIYA HAHTA NASHOBA

I wanted to find out more about my DNA so I decided I want to find my cousins so we can make the link on our family tree so I tested with 23andme so I could find my family it was one of the best choices I have ever made.

I found my cousin Amber on 23andme come to find out my Great Grandfather and her Great Grandfather x2 are brothers this is my Cherokee line via Virginia, Tennessee and Kentucky.

I have also found two 4th cousins who are half Korean neither of them are directly related to each other I am related to both of them via my Great Uncles time in the Army actually there are a ton of Korean children who were left behind by their American fathers, both women are related to me on my paternal side one through my American Indian Uncle and one through my European Uncle.

I have talked to so many of my cousins I found cousins from Haiti, Ireland, Mexico, Puerto Rico, etc.

Talking to these cousins have helped fill in gaps in my genealogy

I have spoken to my European cousins (Irish, British) they all have been nothing but welcoming and many of them have given me access to the family tree so we can find our common ancestor.

A JOURNEY BACK TO MY INDIGENOUS ROOTS BY ZAKIYA HAHTA NASHOBA

I have also spoken to one of my Puerto Rican cousins whose Grandma is 90 years old and is living back on the Island, we are related on my maternal side.

I spoke to my Haitian cousin she lives in the states she told me about where her parents came from, we are still searching for that grandparent we share in common, I haven't spoken to any of my Dominican cousins yet I have ancestry from Hispaniola not just one side of the Island.

I have used cousin matches to help guide me to what genealogical records I need to search, for example I need to research the records in Puerto Rico and Mexico because I have cousins from my mother's side and my father's side who is Puerto Rican, I also have cousins who are from Mexico this is where my Mayan and Taino ancestry comes from all of these cousins share a common grandparent with me.

I also have California Indian ancestry via the Miwok, Ohlone, and Costanoan (Maternal side)

One of my surnames is battle I was able to reach out to my cousin via DNA match and confirm our connection via the

A JOURNEY BACK TO MY INDIGENOUS ROOTS BY ZAKIYA HAHTA NASHOBA

Seminole tribe, her Grandmother surname Battle is a part of the Seminole tribe in Florida.

I am still searching for the Grandmother we share in common, my great grandmother x4 is Harriet Battle.

I am a walking history book, being Ancient to the Americas my blood tells the story of my people from time immemorial.

I have British, German and Iberian ancestry via Colonization and immigration

I have Irish ancestry via Irish immigration to the Americas some by way of coffin ships (Irish slaves)

I have Jewish ancestry via my great-grandmother x 4 Celia Gimble from Alabama.

My Mother side and Father side is also Cherokee, Lumbee, Creek, Mayan and Choctaw.

My Great Great grandmother on my mother's mother (my Grandma) father's (My Great Grandpa) mother side (my Great Great Grandma) is Elmina Locklear (did I confuse you?)

Elmina Locklear married Matthew Wilkerson

A JOURNEY BACK TO MY INDIGENOUS ROOTS BY ZAKIYA HAHTA NASHOBA

Elmina Locklear father is John Locklear he was born in North Carolina and died in Georgia where my Great Great Grandma Elmina Locklear was born, this is my Lumbee line.

Growing up I remember my Mother telling me that her Grandmother x2 married an Indian and went to live with him in his village at the time the family didn't like him but her Great-grandmother x2 loved him so much she left home at 15 and married him they had 15 children together.

Years later my eldest cousin tells me you know our grandma is Indian I said yea Lumbee (which is Cherokee and Tuscarora)

Talking to people on this journey I find that many so-called African Americans have similar stories to tell, almost everyone knows of their Indian ancestry but it got pushed to the side for black pride.

I also have ancestry from Jamaica (Arawak/Taino)

Puerto Rico (Taino) Mexico (Mayan) and Cuba (Taino) via my maternal side prior to colonization and false borders it was normal for us to travel from the mainland to the various islands.

A JOURNEY BACK TO MY INDIGENOUS ROOTS BY ZAKIYA HAHTA NASHOBA

I have indigenous Australian roots from my Father's side

I must note that the previously mentioned names are a colonized interpretation of the indigenous population's post-Columbus I use them for the sake of familiarity and ease of comprehension.

I have only scratched the surface of my many connections to the global family of indigenous peoples.

I know that all my connections whether it be from the Americas or Europe all lead back to an indigenous dark skin root.

I want to take a moment to share with you some pictures of my Parent's and Grand Parents.

A JOURNEY BACK TO MY INDIGENOUS ROOTS BY ZAKIYA HAHTA NASHOBA

My mother Linda

A JOURNEY BACK TO MY INDIGENOUS ROOTS BY ZAKIYA HAHTA NASHOBA

My Dad James his nickname as a child was little Aborigine

A JOURNEY BACK TO MY INDIGENOUS ROOTS BY ZAKIYA HAHTA NASHOBA

Maternal side

This is my grandmother Maeval Wilkerson and my grandfather Thomas Stevens

A JOURNEY BACK TO MY INDIGENOUS ROOTS BY ZAKIYA HAHTA NASHOBA

This is Thomas Stevens father Thomas Stevens Sr my great grandfather

A JOURNEY BACK TO MY INDIGENOUS ROOTS BY ZAKIYA HAHTA NASHOBA

My Paternal side

This is my Grandmother Marylene Love

I am kin to Nate Love (the famous cowboy) via this grandmother.

A JOURNEY BACK TO MY INDIGENOUS ROOTS BY ZAKIYA HAHTA NASHOBA

Andrew Robinson and Catherine Robinson from Kentucky (right)

A JOURNEY BACK TO MY INDIGENOUS ROOTS BY ZAKIYA HAHTA NASHOBA

PART II: My Journey

My Journey into decolonizing my bloodline was not an easy journey at all, I fell ill from the stress of finding out exactly what happened to my people.

I called a family meeting to discuss with my family how we had been renamed, I showed my family genetic and genealogy records of our indigenous ancestry.

I received some resistance from my older Christianized cousins who believed in the whole African Slavery narrative and had based their lives off of it, it was only when I told them that if my Grandmother is Indigenous and your Mother is my Grandmother's sister then that makes you Indigenous at that point they remembered the story of one of my Maternal Grandmothers being stolen away by a Lumbee Indian.

A JOURNEY BACK TO MY INDIGENOUS ROOTS BY ZAKIYA HAHTA NASHOBA

My family decided that since I had been the one called forward by our ancestors to discover what happened to our family that I would be the Chief of our Tribe so that I could ensure that our future generations would never forget who they are.

I thanked them for honoring me with the title and began to go to work decolonizing our bloodline.

I was on what felt like my death bed when my ancestors woke me at 5 am to write a letter to the President of the U.S

I woke up and wrote the letter and mailed it the same day

I will insert pictures of the first letter and the subsequent letters so that it is easy to follow along.

I omitted my address for privacy and safety.

A JOURNEY BACK TO MY INDIGENOUS ROOTS BY ZAKIYA HAHTA NASHOBA

Dear Mr. President
certified# 7018 0040 0000 5249 1876

Halito (Hello) and well wishes for you and your family.

I am corresponding with you on a matter that is urgent and of great importance to my family.

Allow me to properly introduce myself I am Chief Zakiya Hahta Nashoba of the Yazoo Choctaw Nation my bloodline is of the oldest inhabitants of what we now call A me ri ca (known to most as America).

I am from the most Ancient of Ancients my people did not cross the land bridge we have always been on the continent of A me ri ca (America) since time immemorial, our skin is as deep and dark as the most fertile soil that springs forth life.

I have been directed to write you this letter in honor of my ancestors and future descendants.

Many of my forefathers have served the U.S in the many wars for freedom and fought alongside many soldiers that did not see them as worthy to breathe yet they fought with honor and endured all forms of discrimination and their sons fought with honor and endured the same.

My foremothers endured great hardships as their ancient customs and ancient lands were taken from them yet they remained strong and endured great discrimination and genocidal acts.

My foremothers and forefathers survived long enough to give life to the people who gave life to me so I must honor them.

A JOURNEY BACK TO MY INDIGENOUS ROOTS BY ZAKIYA HAHTA NASHOBA

A great deal of my bloodline is from the territory of the Powhatan Confederacy now called Virginia/Kentucky.

I also have a Great Great Great Grandfather who came to the colony of Jamestown from Europe to live as most people say the American Dream, I honor him also although his actions oppressed my ancient peoples he is still my blood and I will not deny him.

Because of policies put into place at Jamestown and later with Walter Plecker my people endured paper genocide, Financial genocide, loss of liberty, loss of ancient customs, loss of Tribal affiliations and Loss of their lands without land you have no wealth and no means to successfully support yourself or future generations.

My people became various forms of false and foreign designations such as Colored, Black, Mulatto, White (If their skin was fair enough) and now this thing called African American which confuses my people.

We have come out of exile to honor our ancestors and to return to our ancient ways of living, for so long we have been separated from our identities because of policies put into place at the various colonies to honor the ancestors of the settlers who arrived while disgracing my ancestors.

If I may change the subject for a moment and share with you a vision I had.

My ancestors came to me in a form of a White wolf to help guide me on my path to restore the customs and honor of my ancient bloodline as I was feeling fearful of this journey due to ancestral memories of all forms of violent acts towards my ancestors I was comforted in knowing I was doing the right thing and that they will guide me, A year later my ancestors appeared to me as a Black wolf which is my protector on this journey.

I say all that to say I was guided by my ancestors to reach out to you, not to scold you or to blame you but to communicate with you about the concerns of my bloodline.

A JOURNEY BACK TO MY INDIGENOUS ROOTS BY ZAKIYA HAHTA NASHOBA

My people have endured so much in our ancient lands that has caused a fracture in our true identities and have left many confused and just beaten down living day to day waiting to die no one should live like that tears are flowing as I write this letter but I must continue.

My people are kind and generous people we have always been so, we protected our families and helped out anyone who needed help it is our ancient disposition as caretakers of A me ri ca.

I am sure you know of the history of the formation of the U.S and the great battles fought and the genocide that occurred to secure the stronghold of the U.S I will not bore you with the details this letter is not about blaming you.

I will jump straight into the issue my bloodline face as of 4/10/2018.

Due to lost of customs, Identities and Tribal affiliations a condition forced upon us by agents of the colonies i.e. States and in particular an agent that has caused a great deal of harm agent Walter Ashby Plecker with his racial integrity act my people have been illegally taxed your constitution which was influenced by the Iroquois confederacy clearly says Indians not taxed.

100th congress 2d session H.Con.Res. 331.

I bring up the subject of taxation in reference to my bloodline descendants/ascendants of ancient A me ri ca because it has been wrongfully placed upon us we choose to live our ancient Tribal ways. illegal taxation keeps us in a state of poverty simply because as we contract with foreign companies for jobs they mandate that we must fill out a W2 etc. in order to simply do honest work so that we may feed our families the U.S constitution says Indians not taxed.

My ancient Bloodline has endured loss of land we no longer have a parcel to our name to cultivate and live on.

We have been backed in a corner and faced with the choice of live in accordance with our ancient ways and honor our ancestors or

A JOURNEY BACK TO MY INDIGENOUS ROOTS BY ZAKIYA HAHTA NASHOBA

accept the various genocidal instruments that continue to take us away from out true identities such tools as SS#, Birth Certificates and Driver's license just so that we can live another day and feed our families, if we continue this way our future generations will never know who they are.

I work tirelessly every single day picking up the pieces of colonial times.

I am without any income and land yet I must honor my ancestors and continue moving forward.

My future generations are depending upon me to bring us out of the shadows and exile and into the light of our ancient ways to boldly stand and say I am the Ancient One.

Mr. President

How can you help us in the matter of the issues my bloodline face?

It has been 10 years since the implementation of UNDRIP and now we have Adrip yet most colonies i.e. States has not done anything to implement it and if they have we are not aware of what they have done, if you have information on how it has been implemented in the various territories we would greatly appreciate you forwarding that information to us.

On the issue of land my bloodline would greatly appreciate an allotment of land so that we can properly sustain our lives we are dying from lack of land to raise cattle and grow our own food.

Forgive me if my English do not meet the standard format it is a foreign language to me and my people.

In closing my people wish to live in peace and harmony with all of our hereditary rights of liberty given to us by our creators we are the Ancient Ones. Yakoke (Thanks) for taking the time to read my letter we look forward to your response.

Respectfully *Chief Zakiya Hahta Nashoba*

Letter was received April 16, 2018 at 4:00 am Delivered WASHINGTON, DC 20500

A JOURNEY BACK TO MY INDIGENOUS ROOTS BY ZAKIYA HAHTA NASHOBA

United States Department of the Interior
OFFICE OF THE SECRETARY
Washington, DC 20240

JUN 2 2 2018

DTS - IACC001726

Mr. Zakiya Hahta Nashoba

Dear Mr. Nashoba:

Thank you for your material, post marked April 10, 2018, to the President, regarding a group known as the "Yazoo Choctaw Nation." The Department assigned the materials to the Office of Federal Acknowledgment (OFA) within the Office of the Assistant Secretary – Indian Affairs, for response. OFA received your materials on June 18, 2018, and we apologize for the delay in our response.

The OFA works with groups seeking to be federally acknowledged as Indian tribes under Part 83 of Title 25 of the *Code of Federal Regulations* (25 CFR Part 83). Enclosed, please find a copy of 25 CFR Part 83. The Department recently revised these regulations and they became final and effective on July 31, 2015 (2015 regulations). If a group submits a fully "documented petition," meets all the requirements under 25 CFR Part 83, and completes the process, then the Department acknowledges the group as an Indian tribe. The Department then adds the newly acknowledged Indian tribe on the list of "Indian Entities Recognized and Eligible To Receive Services From the United States Bureau of Indian Affairs," pursuant to Federal statute (Federally Recognized Indian Tribe List Act of 1994). The Department publishes this list in the *Federal Register* on an annual basis.

Currently, the Department recognizes 573 federally recognized Indian tribes. The Department, mainly through the Bureau of Indian Affairs, works with the duly elected and authorized elected officials and governing bodies of each of these federally recognized Indian tribes. Your material makes reference to a group known as the "Yazoo Choctaw Nation," however, this group is neither federally recognized nor on the list of federally recognized Indian tribes. You may wish to consider the Federal acknowledgment process under 25 CFR Part 83. Should you have any questions regarding this process, feel free to contact OFA.

Sincerely,

Acting Director, Office of Federal Acknowledgment

Enclosure

A JOURNEY BACK TO MY INDIGENOUS ROOTS BY ZAKIYA HAHTA NASHOBA

Halito! Dear Acting Director of the Office of Federal Acknowledgement

Forgive me I could not read the signature on the letter you sent me or I would address you by name.

Thank you for your response dated 6/22/2018, and your suggestion that we/I seek Federal Recognition.

I am Chief Zakiya Hahta Nashoba of the Yazoo Choctaw Nation not Mr. Zakiya Hahta Nashoba, I am a Chief of my Tribe and I am not a male but a Female in accordance with our Ancient Matriarchal customs.

The letter sent from your office addressed me as Mr. Zakiya Hahta Nashoba, Chief is my title to be addressed as anything else is disrespectful and dismissive of my indigenous rights, the letter also referred to my people as a group we are not a group we are an Indigenous Nation of People.

Nation deals with common ancestry and birth we are bloodline descendants of the Ancient ones, I will not accept being labeled as a group.

It is essential to respect all indigenous peoples and in particular their leaders, I am not sure who composed the response letter to me but they didn't take into account the core element of respect and the right of indigenous people to form their own communities.

A JOURNEY BACK TO MY INDIGENOUS ROOTS BY ZAKIYA HAHTA NASHOBA

My reason for not seeking Federal recognition is based on the fact that we/I don't need Federal Recognition to be who we/I am and that's Indigenous and Autochthonous to A me ri ca (The Continent).

My people existed millions of years before such a concept of being Federally recognized and in my Ancient customs it is the Elder that recognizes the Youth and give their blessing, my people are the Elder and this recognition process is the youth.

I dare not disturbed the Ancient order of doing things and disgrace my ancestors by seeking Federal Recognition.

Furthermore, the current system of Federal Recognition is a demoralizing experience for indigenous people it is set up to make people feel as if they are not worthy unless they achieve this thing called Federal Recognition.

I understand that many Native Tribes are satisfied with the fact they are Federally Recognized but for me and my people we choose to live how we lived before such a system was put into place to divide and conquer our people, Federally Recognized versus Non-Federally Recognized.

There has been important meetings in Washington that has excluded Indigenous Peoples because they are not Federally Recognized I don't see how such a system would be in the best interest of Indigenous Peoples.

The Federal Recognition process is not viable nor is it realistic for the vast majority of indigenous peoples who have endured paper genocide, relocation and separation from their Tribes.

One of the requirements is to show existence as an Indian Tribe before 1900 now this requirement is just not in accordance with historical facts, in the 1600's many Tribes had their people enslaved for resisting the colonist this started a long process of enslavement and paper

A JOURNEY BACK TO MY INDIGENOUS ROOTS BY ZAKIYA HAHTA NASHOBA

genocide, In the 1800's many locations that held important historical documents was burned to the ground removing all evidence of indigenous people owning land and inhabiting certain regions in Colonial times.

Colonist was in charge and determining who was worthy and who was not, (very reminiscent of this Federal recognition system) indigenous people were not deemed worthy in their eyes so they destroyed anything that would show that indigenous people were not some poor child needing the help of the "Great White father".

Many Tribes who have chosen to seek Federal Recognition have been waiting for decades to be approved and some have been waiting for 130 years, imagine the psychological damage they are suffering in the process.

I dare not cause my people to suffer in such a way we have endured enough suffering since Colonization.

We are still dealing with the effects of Colonization and Genocide my people cannot handle the demeaning process of Federal recognition we are already in a fragile state.

I am very curious to how Federal Recognition deals with the effects of paper genocide since the entire process deals with a continuous paper trail, understanding this will help me grasp the concept of Federal recognition for people of paper genocide such as my people.

In such a situation where there has been paper genocide and reclassification and the loss of Nationality i.e. Tribal Affiliation how could victims of such atrocities possibly meet all the criteria of Federal Recognition?

How would that be better then being historically recognized, recognized by my community and recognized by blood?

A JOURNEY BACK TO MY INDIGENOUS ROOTS BY ZAKIYA HAHTA NASHOBA

What would be the advantage of Federal Recognition and how is it different from colonization?

In closing let me say that land is essential to the survival of any species and as it currently stands My People have no land to call their own thus prompting the extinction of my people.

We have inherited the soil by blood (Indigenous title) however due to Colonization it has been stripped from us leaving us in total poverty and landless.

Federal Recognition should not be our only option to ensure our survival.

Indigenous people are more disadvantage then any other population of people, the psychological effects of being stripped of the most basic necessity of Life i.e. land to cultivate and live upon is devasting.

When I speak of land I am talking about fertile soil, no Indigenous person should be suffering homelessness or hunger on the soil they have inhabited since time immemorial, nor should they have to worry about paying rent that is just salt in the wound.

I believe knowledge brings light to a dark situation I would love to have my questions answered so that I may be enlightened.

Forgive me if my letter displayed a since of frustration I am still coping with the effects of genocide and the ongoing process of extinction via loss of land and the disrespect displayed in the initial response letter.

Using my proper title as Chief would have not brought about the problem of addressing me as a man when I am not.

Thank you for your time and I look forward to your response.

Chief Zakiya Hahta Nashoba

A JOURNEY BACK TO MY INDIGENOUS ROOTS BY ZAKIYA HAHTA NASHOBA

United States Department of the Interior
OFFICE OF THE SECRETARY
Washington, DC 20240

JUL 26 2018

Ms. Zakiya Hahta Nashoba
~~[address redacted]~~

Dear Ms. Nashoba:

Thank you for your recent letter. The Office of Federal Acknowledgment received it on July 18, 2018.

Your letter indicated that you are not interested in the Department of the Interior's (Department) revised administrative process for the Federal acknowledgment of Indian tribes that was became effective on July 31, 2018, and is found in Part 83 of Title 25 of the Code of Federal Regulations (25 CFR Part 83). There is no requirement or expectation that you and your group would seek Federal acknowledgment. If, at some point, you change your mind, you are encouraged to visit the Department's Federal acknowledgment website. Currently, that website is available here:

www.bia.gov/as-ia/ofa

Your letter also raised questions regarding the criteria for Federal acknowledgment and the origins of the Department's acknowledgment process. For further information, please visit the "Supplemental Administrative and Regulatory Documents" page on the Department's Federal acknowledgment website:

www.bia.gov/as-ia/ofa/supplemental-administrative-and-regulatory-documents

Generally speaking, when executive agencies of the Federal Government issue a new regulation or revise an existing one, they follow a "rulemaking" process. In the rulemaking process, an agency publishes a "proposed rule" in the *Federal Register* and then accepts comments from the public about the rule. If the public submits comments, the agency evaluates them, modifies the proposed rule accordingly, and issues a "final rule." The first printing of the final rule in the *Federal Register* often contains an introduction that includes a summary of the comments provided by the public, as well as the agency's responses to those comments.

To better understand the Federal acknowledgment process, look for the following links on the "Supplemental Administrative and Regulatory Documents" web page: the "2015 Final Rule," the "Final Rule" for the 1994 revision to the acknowledgment regulations, the "initial 1978 guidelines," the "1977 comments," and the "1978 comments." These links provide extensive information about the formulation of the original acknowledgment regulations published in 1978, as well as about the revisions of the acknowledgment regulations in 1994 and 2015.

A JOURNEY BACK TO MY INDIGENOUS ROOTS BY ZAKIYA HAHTA NASHOBA

In closing, please accept my apologies for addressing our previous letter to "Mr. Zakiya Hahta Nashoba" rather than "Ms. Zakiya Hahta Nashoba." This mistake was purely accidental.

Sincerely,

R. Lee Fleming
Director, Office of Federal Acknowledgment

A JOURNEY BACK TO MY INDIGENOUS ROOTS BY ZAKIYA HAHTA NASHOBA

In true Colonial fashion they refused to honor my indigenous rights and to address me as Chief this is a legal move albeit ineffective.

Notice where they said there is no requirement or expectation to seek Federal Recognition, despite the myth that you must be Federally recognized to be legitimate.

I know just like they know that Federal Recognition turns you into a political and legal Indian who no longer have control over their Tribe.

I will expound further on this topic later in the book.

A JOURNEY BACK TO MY INDIGENOUS ROOTS BY ZAKIYA HAHTA NASHOBA

Chapter Three: My Travels

My research took me to many locations, I was on a mission to honor my Pre-Columbian roots.

First stop was Belize, I traveled across Belize on a chicken bus (old school bus) heading for Xunantunich the ancient Mayan ruins (I believe they are actually Olmec)

I arrived at the site with my travel companion, we decided to hire a local guide not because we needed them but because we decided to help someone make money for the day, I figured why not this is how he feeds his family.

Our guide had been doing this job for 10 years he said the other guides don't like him because he always shows the tourist that the Mayans had locs in their head (misnomer dreadlocks)

Our guide was cool I was able to show him some stuff he hadn't even noticed before, I was simply using my inherited Ancient Knowledge of the land, I remember on the way back down the steep hill I decided not to walk on the asphalt the guide said to me that it would be easier if I did,

A JOURNEY BACK TO MY INDIGENOUS ROOTS BY ZAKIYA HAHTA NASHOBA

I told him to step onto the grass you will feel an immediate shift, you will notice that walking downhill you have a better center of gravity he tried it and was amazed just how easy it was to walk on the grass where he could be grounded.

As we walked down the hill, I started to point out to him the faces carved on the side of the road, he said wow! I never saw that before I told him they cut this road straight through an Ancient courtyard.

I traveled to the Olmec site Lamanai to see the large Negroid faces, the guide there told me there were seven faces each one representing a ruler, five have been removed only two remains.

I noticed at all the sites I traveled to in Belize, Guatemala and Honduras all of the Pyramids have been disturbed it looks as if whatever overlay that was on them had been removed.

A JOURNEY BACK TO MY INDIGENOUS ROOTS BY ZAKIYA HAHTA NASHOBA

Left to right

My eldest daughter Shi'ra, Me, Jzoe on the back row left to right is Gary aka LSD next to him is Blunts these are my Belizeans Garifuna travel companions.

A JOURNEY BACK TO MY INDIGENOUS ROOTS BY ZAKIYA HAHTA NASHOBA

A JOURNEY BACK TO MY INDIGENOUS ROOTS BY ZAKIYA HAHTA NASHOBA

Lamanai Mask Temple

A JOURNEY BACK TO MY INDIGENOUS ROOTS BY ZAKIYA HAHTA NASHOBA

A JOURNEY BACK TO MY INDIGENOUS ROOTS BY ZAKIYA HAHTA NASHOBA

Blunts he is Garifuna from Belize

A JOURNEY BACK TO MY INDIGENOUS ROOTS BY ZAKIYA HAHTA NASHOBA

A JOURNEY BACK TO MY INDIGENOUS ROOTS BY ZAKIYA HAHTA NASHOBA

A JOURNEY BACK TO MY INDIGENOUS ROOTS BY ZAKIYA HAHTA NASHOBA

My daughter Shi'ra and Jzoe at Lamanai in Belize sitting on top of the structure.

A JOURNEY BACK TO MY INDIGENOUS ROOTS BY ZAKIYA HAHTA NASHOBA

A JOURNEY BACK TO MY INDIGENOUS ROOTS BY ZAKIYA HAHTA NASHOBA

This waterfall is amazing

A JOURNEY BACK TO MY INDIGENOUS ROOTS BY ZAKIYA HAHTA NASHOBA

I saw this guy with this amazing hat, he is Q'eqchi' Maya if only you could see all the red, orange, yellow, blue and green in the Exotic bird feathers.

A JOURNEY BACK TO MY INDIGENOUS ROOTS BY ZAKIYA HAHTA NASHOBA

A JOURNEY BACK TO MY INDIGENOUS ROOTS BY ZAKIYA HAHTA NASHOBA

A JOURNEY BACK TO MY INDIGENOUS ROOTS BY ZAKIYA HAHTA NASHOBA

A JOURNEY BACK TO MY INDIGENOUS ROOTS BY ZAKIYA HAHTA NASHOBA

He allowed all of us to take a picture with his hat

A JOURNEY BACK TO MY INDIGENOUS ROOTS BY ZAKIYA HAHTA NASHOBA

A JOURNEY BACK TO MY INDIGENOUS ROOTS BY ZAKIYA HAHTA NASHOBA

I saw this couple and I said hey family let's take a group photo

A JOURNEY BACK TO MY INDIGENOUS ROOTS BY ZAKIYA HAHTA NASHOBA

Tikal in Guatemala

A JOURNEY BACK TO MY INDIGENOUS ROOTS BY ZAKIYA HAHTA NASHOBA

A JOURNEY BACK TO MY INDIGENOUS ROOTS BY ZAKIYA HAHTA NASHOBA

A JOURNEY BACK TO MY INDIGENOUS ROOTS BY ZAKIYA HAHTA NASHOBA

Tikal in guatemaya (Gautemala)

A JOURNEY BACK TO MY INDIGENOUS ROOTS BY ZAKIYA HAHTA NASHOBA

A JOURNEY BACK TO MY INDIGENOUS ROOTS BY ZAKIYA HAHTA NASHOBA

A JOURNEY BACK TO MY INDIGENOUS ROOTS BY ZAKIYA HAHTA NASHOBA

A JOURNEY BACK TO MY INDIGENOUS ROOTS BY ZAKIYA HAHTA NASHOBA

A JOURNEY BACK TO MY INDIGENOUS ROOTS BY ZAKIYA HAHTA NASHOBA

A JOURNEY BACK TO MY INDIGENOUS ROOTS BY ZAKIYA HAHTA NASHOBA

A JOURNEY BACK TO MY INDIGENOUS ROOTS BY ZAKIYA HAHTA NASHOBA

A JOURNEY BACK TO MY INDIGENOUS ROOTS BY ZAKIYA HAHTA NASHOBA

A JOURNEY BACK TO MY INDIGENOUS ROOTS BY ZAKIYA HAHTA NASHOBA

A JOURNEY BACK TO MY INDIGENOUS ROOTS BY ZAKIYA HAHTA NASHOBA

A JOURNEY BACK TO MY INDIGENOUS ROOTS BY ZAKIYA HAHTA NASHOBA

A JOURNEY BACK TO MY INDIGENOUS ROOTS BY ZAKIYA HAHTA NASHOBA

A JOURNEY BACK TO MY INDIGENOUS ROOTS BY ZAKIYA HAHTA NASHOBA

A JOURNEY BACK TO MY INDIGENOUS ROOTS BY ZAKIYA HAHTA NASHOBA

A JOURNEY BACK TO MY INDIGENOUS ROOTS BY ZAKIYA HAHTA NASHOBA

Iximiche Guatemala this circle is POWERFUL

I noticed at this site the ground sparkled like little flecks of glitter

A JOURNEY BACK TO MY INDIGENOUS ROOTS BY ZAKIYA HAHTA NASHOBA

My Travels in Honduras in the mountains with the Chorti Maya

A JOURNEY BACK TO MY INDIGENOUS ROOTS BY ZAKIYA HAHTA NASHOBA

Chorti Maya woman she liked my hair so I braided hers

A JOURNEY BACK TO MY INDIGENOUS ROOTS BY ZAKIYA HAHTA NASHOBA

A JOURNEY BACK TO MY INDIGENOUS ROOTS BY ZAKIYA HAHTA NASHOBA

Miskito Indian man and child in Honduras with Jzoe and I

A JOURNEY BACK TO MY INDIGENOUS ROOTS BY ZAKIYA HAHTA NASHOBA

Copan Honduras

A JOURNEY BACK TO MY INDIGENOUS ROOTS BY ZAKIYA HAHTA NASHOBA

Chapter Four: Urban Myth

Urban Myths and how it keeps people from speaking, seeing and hearing the truth.

In a world where we don't talk about the truth because we care more about making people feel comfortable with lies, I have decided to speak my truth regardless of who it makes uncomfortable.

A JOURNEY BACK TO MY INDIGENOUS ROOTS BY ZAKIYA HAHTA NASHOBA

Urban myth #1

"The Five Civilized Tribes"

In order to destroy this urban myth, we must first take a moment to look at what civilized means to the European immigrants who played a role in the theft of our ancient lands and the murdering of my people.

"Civilized" means a Nation who has agreed to bow before the Holy See and give all power and authority over to the Christian God and its Vicars.

We did NOT WORSHIP ANY CHRISTIAN GODS BEFORE the Immigrant Europeans arrived.

This decision by the "Five Civilized" tribes cost them dearly, in 1906 their entire Government was no more

A JOURNEY BACK TO MY INDIGENOUS ROOTS BY ZAKIYA HAHTA NASHOBA

" CHEROKEES.

"ART. 5. The United States hereby covenants and agrees that tl lands ceded to the Cherokee Nation in the foregoing article shall in future time, without their consent, be included within the territori limits or jurisdiction of any State or Territory." (Revised Indi Treaties, p. 69.)

Similar treaties with the other four tribes were also made.

I have been unable to find any treaties that abrogate thes treaties, and I am unable to find any law which would abroga them by implication. I should like to know what the Senator view is in regard to whether those treaties have been abrogate

Mr. STEWART. Yes; they have been abrogated.

Mr. NELSON. If the Senator from Nevada will allow me, desire to state to the Senator from Georgia that these o treaties to which the House committee refer have been pract cally abrogated by subsequent treaties and negotiations mad with the Indians under the so-called "Curtis Act" of 189 That act and the treaties which were entered into under it ar the subsequent act ratifying those treaties have practical repealed and taken the place of those old treaties to which refers.

Mr. CLAY. I would ask the Senator——

Mr. NELSON. The Senator will allow me?

Mr. CLAY. Certainly.

Mr. NELSON. The Senator will find a history of this matte and of these treaties, as well as the decisions of the court bea ing upon it, in the remarks I made two years ago, on pages 2 24, and 25, where I have gone in great detail into this matter.

Mr. STEWART. The result is understood thoroughly. Tl Indians agreed to the allotment of their lands. The treati were made with them by the Dawes Commission, and there hav been subsequent treaties made, and they have all agreed tha the tribal relation shall be dissolved on the 4th of March, 190

Mr. CLAY. Then the Senator thinks that the simple fa that the Indians have agreed to have their lands allotted ar the tribal relations dissolved would abrogate the treaty pr

A JOURNEY BACK TO MY INDIGENOUS ROOTS BY ZAKIYA HAHTA NASHOBA

Mr. CLAY. Certainly.

Mr. NELSON. The Senator will find a history of this matter and of these treaties, as well as the decisions of the court bearing upon it, in the remarks I made two years ago, on pages 22, 24, and 25, where I have gone in great detail into this matter.

Mr. STEWART. The result is understood thoroughly. The Indians agreed to the allotment of their lands. The treaties were made with them by the Dawes Commission, and there have been subsequent treaties made, and they have all agreed that the tribal relation shall be dissolved on the 4th of March, 1906.

Mr. CLAY. Then the Senator thinks that the simple fact that the Indians have agreed to have their lands allotted and the tribal relations dissolved would abrogate the treaty providing that their territory should not be formed into a State hereafter without their consent?

Mr. STEWART. Absolutely, because they are individuals and no longer in tribal relation.

Mr. CLAY. I think it is exceedingly doubtful.

Mr. STEWART. The United States has a right to legislate for all white and Indian individuals in the United States. Congress further has the right, according to my view of the it has the power to do it. It is the duty of the United States to take care of the Indians, because they have agreed that their tribal relations shall be dissolved, and Congress must provide some government for them. It has become a duty to do so since the Indians have agreed to the dissolution of their tribal relation.

Mr. BEVERIDGE. In other words, the treaty was between this Government and the tribes.

Mr. STEWART. Yes.

Mr. BEVERIDGE. The existence of this entity, called "the tribes," was a matter among its members. These members agreed to the dissolution of the tribal relation, and the entity with which the treaty was made went out of existence. Does not the Senator from Georgia see that any agreement made with

A JOURNEY BACK TO MY INDIGENOUS ROOTS BY ZAKIYA HAHTA NASHOBA

this Government and the tribes.

Mr. STEWART. Yes.

Mr. BEVERIDGE. The existence of this entity, called "the tribes," was a matter among its members. These members agreed to the dissolution of the tribal relation, and the entity with which the treaty was made went out of existence. Does not the Senator from Georgia see that any agreement made with an entity which itself went out of existence of its own volition of course ceases by that very act? Otherwise before anything could ever be done in the history of the world that involved these Indians who ceased to be a tribe and became individuals, you would have to get the consent of each individual one of them, which of course is unthinkable.

Mr. STEWART. They have done that in some cases by vote.

Mr. BEVERIDGE. But not in the case the Senator referred to.

Mr. STEWART. No.

Mr. CLAY. These lands have not yet been allotted. The allotment will not be completed before 1906.

Mr. BEVERIDGE. My remarks were not directed to that phase of it, but to that phase of the Senator's question which forms its second part, which was that treaties inhibited the joining of their lands into any State government without their consent.

Mr. CLAY. Yes.

Mr. BEVERIDGE. The Senator from Nevada answered that by saying the tribal relations had been abolished, and then I asked the Senator if it did not become perfectly apparent to him that it abolished any agreement of that kind.

Mr. CLAY. It might do it by implication.

Mr. BEVERIDGE. Absolutely.

Mr. CLAY. That act has not been carried out. The allotment will not be completed until 1906.

A JOURNEY BACK TO MY INDIGENOUS ROOTS BY ZAKIYA HAHTA NASHOBA

> Mr. BEVERIDGE. The Senator asked two questions. The one involved land, and the other involved the consent of the tribes to incorporating their territory into a State. That is the second portion, and it is to that portion of the Senator's question that I am addressing this interruption.
>
> Mr. CLAY. I understand the Senator to say, then, that there is no direct legislation or treaty abrogating the treaties to which I have referred. You simply take into consideration the Curtis Act, which provides for the allotment of these lands, and then when they are alloted, you say by implication the Indians become citizens——
>
> Mr. BEVERIDGE. No.
>
> Mr. CLAY. And that they consent that their tribal relations shall be dissolved, and by implication the treaties are abrogated?
>
> Mr. STEWART. They have consented by these treaties to become individuals the same as you and I.
>
> Mr. BEVERIDGE. Certainly.
>
> Mr. STEWART. They have voted to become individuals, and now it becomes the duty of the United States to provide a government for them.
>
> Mr. BEVERIDGE. Before that they were not individuals. Before that they were portions of an entity called a tribe, with which entity this Government made the treaty. As to whether that entity should continue of course was a question for its members. Its members ceased to be a tribe, and became individuals of their own volition. Is that a correct statement?
>
> Mr. STEWART. That is a correct statement, and that is the fact. Before this law takes effect the tribes will all be out of existence. The State is not to be admitted until after the tribal relation is dissolved under the law.
>
> Mr. BEVERIDGE. Exactly; and in the original bill that fact was taken into consideration and a date was fixed far enough ahead——
>
> Mr. CLAY. You mean that the statehood bill will not take effect until 1906?

One year later the political territory called Indian country aka Oklahoma was created over 70 years after indigenous peoples were forced out west and placed in what we now know as Oklahoma.

A JOURNEY BACK TO MY INDIGENOUS ROOTS BY ZAKIYA HAHTA NASHOBA

Let's take a look at the term that has been used in this congressional record, the word is DISSOLUTION

mid-14c., "frivolity, moral laxness, dissolute living;" late 14c., *dissolucioun*, "separation into parts, dispersal;" from Old French *dissolution* (12c.) and directly from Latin *dissolutionem* (nominative *dissolutio*) "a dissolving, destroying, interruption, dissolution," noun of action from past participle stem of *dissolvere* "to loosen up, break apart" (see dissolve).

Source: for the dissolving of the Five CIVILIZED Tribes Congressional records

https://www.loc.gov/law/help/statutes-at-large/59th-congress/session-1/c59s1ch1876.pdf

Take a look at one of many edicts by the Catholic/Christian order.

Source: https://www.gilderlehrman.org/sites/default/files/inline-pdfs/T-04093.pdf

A JOURNEY BACK TO MY INDIGENOUS ROOTS BY ZAKIYA HAHTA NASHOBA

Pope Alexander VI. Demarcation Bull Granting Spain Possession of Lands Discovered by Columbus, Rome, May 4, 1493.

Excerpt

Alexander, bishop, servant of the servants of God, to the illustrious sovereigns, our very dear son in Christ, Ferdinand, king, and our very dear daughter in Christ, Isabella, queen of Castile, Leon, Aragon, Sicily, and Granada, health and apostolic benediction.

Among other works well pleasing to the Divine Majesty and cherished of our heart, this assuredly ranks highest, that in our times especially the **Catholic faith** and the **Christian religion** be exalted and be **everywhere increased** and spread, that the health of souls be cared for and **that barbarous nations be overthrown** and **brought to the faith itself**.

Wherefore in as- much as by the favor of divine clemency, we, though of insufficient merits, have been called to this Holy See of Peter, recognizing that as true **Catholic kings and princes**, such as we have known you always to be and as your illustrious

A JOURNEY BACK TO MY INDIGENOUS ROOTS BY ZAKIYA HAHTA NASHOBA

deeds already are known to almost the whole world declare, you not only eagerly desire but with

every effort, zeal, and diligence, without regard to hardships, expenses, dangers, with the shedding even of your blood, are laboring to that end; recognizing also that you have long since

dedicated to this purpose your whole soul and all your endeavors--as witnessed in these times with so much glory to the Divine Name in your recovery of the kingdom of Granada from the yoke of the Saracens--we therefore are rightly led, and hold it as our duty, to grant you even of our own accord and in your favor those things whereby with effort each day more hearty you

may be enabled for the **honor of God** himself and **the spread of the Christian rule** to carry forward your holy and praiseworthy purpose so pleasing to immortal God. We have indeed learned that you, who for a long time had intended to **seek out and discover certain islands and mainland's remote and unknown** and not hitherto discovered by others, to the end that you might **bring to the worship of our Redeemer and the profession of the Catholic faith** their residents and

A JOURNEY BACK TO MY INDIGENOUS ROOTS BY ZAKIYA HAHTA NASHOBA

inhabitants, having been up to the present time greatly engaged in the siege and recovery of the kingdom itself of Granada were unable to accomplish this holy and praiseworthy purpose; but

the said kingdom having at length been regained, as was **pleasing to the Lord**, you, with the wish to fulfill your desire, chose our beloved son, Christopher Columbus, a man assuredly worthy and

of the highest recommendations and fitted for so great an undertaking, whom you furnished with

ships and men equipped for like designs, not without the greatest hardships, dangers, and expenses, to make diligent quest for these remote and unknown mainland's and islands through

the sea, where hitherto no one had sailed; and they at length, with divine aid and with the utmost diligence sailing in the ocean sea, discovered certain very remote islands and even mainland's that hitherto had not been discovered by others; wherein dwell very many peoples **living in peace**, and, as reported, going unclothed, and **not eating flesh**.

Moreover, as your aforesaid envoys are of opinion, these very peoples living in the said islands and countries believe in one

A JOURNEY BACK TO MY INDIGENOUS ROOTS BY ZAKIYA HAHTA NASHOBA

God, the Creator in heaven, and **seem sufficiently disposed to embrace the Catholic faith and be**

trained in good morals. And it is hoped that were **they instructed, the name of the Savior, our**

Lord Jesus Christ, would easily be **introduced** into the said countries and islands. Also, on one of the chiefs of these aforesaid islands the said Christopher has already caused to be put together and built a fortress fairly equipped, wherein he has stationed as garrison certain Christians,

companions of his, who are to make a search for other remote and unknown islands and mainlands. In the islands and countries already discovered are found gold, spices, and very many

other precious things of diverse kinds and qualities. Wherefore, as becomes Catholic kings and princes, after earnest consideration of all matters, especially of **the rise and spread of the Catholic**

faith, as was the fashion of your ancestors, kings of renowned memory, you have purposed with the favor of divine clemency to bring under your sway the said mainland's and islands with their

A JOURNEY BACK TO MY INDIGENOUS ROOTS BY ZAKIYA HAHTA NASHOBA

residents and inhabitants and to bring them to the Catholic faith. Hence, heartily commending in the Lord this your holy and praiseworthy purpose, and desirous that it be duly accomplished, and that the name of our Savior be carried into those regions, we exhort you very earnestly in the

Lord and by your reception of holy baptism, whereby you are bound to our apostolic commands,

and by the bowels of the mercy of our Lord Jesus Christ

A JOURNEY BACK TO MY INDIGENOUS ROOTS BY ZAKIYA HAHTA NASHOBA

Chapter Five: Not "GOOD" enough

*Your skin is "too dark".

(The skin of the Ancients is darker than mine)

*Your hair is "too curly".

(My hair coils like the spiral of life)

*You don't "look Native American"

(My people were on the continent of the Americas BEFORE the migration of the Siberians)

*You don't "live on a reservation".

(My Grandparents escaped imprisonment and stayed behind in our ancestral territory)

*Your grandparents are "not on the rolls".

(The "ROLLS" are inventory of prisoners of war, mandated from the WAR DEPT of the U.S to live in a prison camp called a reservation, it is no different than placing animals on a reservation for the entertainment of others, You had IMMIGRANT EUROPEANS who are very prejudiced deciding who got on the rolls and who was rejected, they placed their families on the rolls because they desired to take even more land by way of Indian land allotments, they also introduced other ethnic groups on the reservation who were NOT Indian in hopes that they would change the phenotype of the original Negroid stock by bottlenecking the genetics.

A JOURNEY BACK TO MY INDIGENOUS ROOTS BY ZAKIYA HAHTA NASHOBA

The threat of losing tribal "STATUS" from having a child outside of the reservation provided an environment for eugenics and the successful breeding out of the Ancient deep dark skin color, Hair texture and common facial features, we have seen this same tactic occurring in Brazil where the Government shipped in IMMIGRANT EUROPEANS to whiten up Brazil which is the site of the most ancient Negroid type, this is where Luzia was found she is 12,000 years old and counting.

Brazil is not the only country that used these eugenic tactics Cuba, Jamaica, South Africa, Australia etc. utilized this system of whitening up the peoples.

The colony of Jamestown nearly failed due to the lack of European women in the colony, the men only had children with indigenous women almost causing the downfall of the colony, this is why they imported IMMIGRANT EUROPEAN women into the colony, they are known as tobacco wives.

THE
"TOBACCO WIVES"

"IF ANY MAID OR SINGLE WOMAN HAVE A DESIRE TO GO OVER, THEY WILL THINK THEMSELVES IN THE GOLDEN AGE, WHEN MEN PAID A DOWRY FOR THEIR WIVES; FOR IF THEY BE BUT CIVIL AND UNDER 50 YEARS OF AGE, SOME HONEST MAN OR OTHER WILL PURCHASE THEM FOR THEIR WIVES"

ADVERTISEMENT PLACED BY SOUTH CAROLINA COLONY (1666)

A JOURNEY BACK TO MY INDIGENOUS ROOTS BY ZAKIYA HAHTA NASHOBA

Sex trafficking was practiced in the colony yet these men are praised in the history books, many of these tobacco wives were young underage girls kidnapped on the streets of Europe.

*You" look African".

(I look American, dark skin and curly hair is not exclusive to the continent of Africa)

*Your Tribe is not "Federally Recognized"

I don't want to relinquish my indigenous autochthonous status by pleading to European IMMIGRANTS for recognition, I don't need European acceptance I am decolonizing my life.

*I never "heard of your Tribe"

(My existence is not dependent upon whether you have heard of my tribe or not, I exist because of my ancient ancestors **Not** because of the idea of whether or not someone has "heard" of me.

*How much Indian do you have in you?

(Are you asking me to dissect millions of years of my ancient DNA to satisfy your genocidal system of dividing people into parts?)

*Are you full blood?

(I am full of blood if I was not full of blood, I would be dead)

*You only have a "little Indian in you"

(Are you implying that I only have one indigenous grandparent?

115

A JOURNEY BACK TO MY INDIGENOUS ROOTS BY ZAKIYA HAHTA NASHOBA

That would be impossible because that Grandparent would have had parents and their parents would have had parents into affinity)

*Are you a "Black Indian"?

(Why are you utilizing genocidal terms to separate me from my ancient roots?

Why are you so preoccupied with the color of my beautiful skin?)

I retain the color of the ancients and I am not ashamed of it, I will not label myself as anything other than ancient, I am a reflection of the beautiful rich soil here on my ancestral land of the Americas to include her beautiful Islands.

* No matter how much evidence you provide or how intelligent you speak, too ignorant people (Lack of knowledge) you will never be "good enough" because you do not fit the image of the lie and genocidal programming that is taught globally.

A JOURNEY BACK TO MY INDIGENOUS ROOTS BY ZAKIYA HAHTA NASHOBA

Many descendants of the Choctaw, Chickasaw, Cherokee, Creek, and Seminole Tribes have gone to these "Civilized" tribes just to be turned away and left to feel like their family (Tribe) didn't want them.

To the people who endured this I am sorry you had to feel this pain let my ease that pain with an explanation as to why you were turned away, in 1906 those Tribes who desired to be civilized and took land allotments no longer was in control of their government.

Essentially you went to Jim Crow asking to be accepted.

Let me include a law put into place for them so it will help you understand.

§199. Access to records of Five Civilized Tribes

The Secretary of the Interior, or his accredited representative, shall at all times have access to any books and records of the Choctaw, Chickasaw, Cherokee, Creek, and Seminole Tribes, whether in possession of any of the officers of either of said tribes or any officer or custodian thereof, of the State of Oklahoma.

(Mar. 1, 1907, ch. 2285, 34 Stat. 1027.)

Ryan Zinke is the current Secretary of Interior

You may ask why is a so called Sovereign Indian Nation mandated to give access to the U.S?

A JOURNEY BACK TO MY INDIGENOUS ROOTS BY ZAKIYA HAHTA NASHOBA

The answer is simple they agreed to this after all you cannot be civilized unless you give up full control of your tribe aka Federally recognized.

I do not pity them they made their bed now they must lie in it.

We often hear the term Government to Government relationship in reference to Indians however that is incorrect it is actually Government to Government only for Federally recognized tribes and why wouldn't it be it's like having a conversation with themselves.

By contract the U.S controls and owns the Five Civilized tribes all finances are controlled by Europeans and their Chiefs are pretty much European basically the higher up the ladder the more European they are just ask the tribal members of these tribes they have many complaints and concerns about money allotment, healthcare etc.

Often when these tribes are needed to perform and act like indigenous peoples in North America are being treated fairly, they come out smile take pictures and shuck and jive.

They have NEVER spoken about indigenous issues they have ALWAYS spoken about corporate issues.

Ask yourself why do these people practice racism against the darker colored Indians when we are the real ancient ones?

I know why it's because we are not "civilized" and not bound by those contracts, they envy us.

A JOURNEY BACK TO MY INDIGENOUS ROOTS BY ZAKIYA HAHTA NASHOBA

On April 7 and 8, 1728, William Byrd visited the town of the Cheroenhaka (Nottoway) Indian Tribe on the tribe's reservation land in what is now Courtland, Virginia. He described how the men and women looked, sang, danced and dressed, the nature of their Fort, Longhouses and bedding; to include, the colors that the women were wearing – Red, White and Blue. Byrd noted in his diary that the Cheroenhaka (Nottoway) Indian Tribe were the only tribe of Indians of any consequence still remaining within the limits of Virginia (not actually true)

Byrd noted that that the Palisade Fort was square about 100 yards on each side. He also described how the young men danced for him with their faces painted, singing and keeping step to the sound of a gore drum stretched tight with an animal skin.

Byrd's papers also note how the women looked in their finery (damsels of old) to include the white and blue couch shell beads in their braided hair and around their necks.

He wrote of the red and blue match coat wrapped loosely around their body that their **mahogany skin** shown through. He also noted that though they be sad colored that they would make great wives for the English planters and that **their dark skin would bleach out in two generations.**

A JOURNEY BACK TO MY INDIGENOUS ROOTS BY ZAKIYA HAHTA NASHOBA

Images are very POWERFUL

The most common mistake people make in researching images of American Indians (misnomer) is looking for Post-Colonial images instead of Pre Columbian artifacts.

Ancient Pre Columbian-peoples did not pose for pictures they showed their images via carvings, etchings, sculpting etc.

Looking at images post-invasion from the 1800s is not an indication of the original peoples who resided here in what we now call America.

DO NOT ALLOW European immigrants to define who is Indigenous to the Americas this is your homeland not theirs we have all seen the great pretenders Iron Eyes Cody (crying Indian) and Frank Dekova among others practiced genocide of imagery sanctioned by their European cohorts and to this day you have people who believe that same imagery because they are still practicing the same old tactic of death by imagery.

Frank DeKova is most known for playing Chief Wild Eagle on F-Troop

More and more archeologist are breaking free from the racist restraints placed upon them and they are speaking out and saying that the Americas was populated by the Negroid BEFORE the arrival of modern Native Americans

A JOURNEY BACK TO MY INDIGENOUS ROOTS BY ZAKIYA HAHTA NASHOBA

The native American Negroes or black Indians, have been seen in Brazil, Guyana, Caraccas, Popayan, Choco, North California, &c. Some of them, such as the Aroras or Caroras of Cumana, were black, but with fine features and long hair, like the Jolofs and Gallas of Africa.

Others in New California, latitude 32, called Esteros, are like the Hottentots, Numuquas, Tambukis, and many other Nigritian tribes, not black, but dark brown, yet complete Negroes, with large thick lips, broad flat noses, and very ugly, with hair crisped or curly.

The Negro features belong to the form of the head rather than the colour, since [there] are in Africa, Asia, and Polynesia, black, brown, yellow, olive, coppery, (and even white) Negroes. May, 1828. C. S. RAFINESQUE.

" The Primitive Black Nations of America." By Professor C. S.Rafinesque.

A JOURNEY BACK TO MY INDIGENOUS ROOTS BY ZAKIYA HAHTA NASHOBA

Ancient Pre-Colombian sites like central Texas (colonial name)

Let me quote an article from Waco Tribune-Herald J.B Smith staff writer Dec 19, 2010

The oldest known man in Central Texas and a girl buried next to him about 11,100 years ago at the Horn Shelter site on the Brazos River are getting new attention as researchers at the Smithsonian Institution analyze their bones and grave goods, and Harvard scientists study their DNA.

Jantz, an expert in skull shapes, said the bones at Horn Shelter

and several other paleo-American sites show little resemblance to modern American Indians, who tend to have round, Asiatic faces.

"The skulls tend to be somewhat longer, narrower and higher than modern Native Americans," he said. "They really don't resemble any modern group very much."

Jantz said the skulls most closely resemble those of Polynesians or the Ainu people of ancient Japan and Manchuria

Ancient Japan, Manchuria, Ainu, and Polynesia were all Negroid types.

A JOURNEY BACK TO MY INDIGENOUS ROOTS BY ZAKIYA HAHTA NASHOBA

NATURAL AND ABORIGINAL

HISTORY

OF

TENNESSEE,

UP TO THE

FIRST SETTLEMENTS THEREIN

BY THE

WHITE PEOPLE,

IN THE

YEAR 1768.

BY JOHN HAYWOOD,

OF THE COUNTY OF DAVIDSON, IN THE STATE OF TENNESSEE.

A JOURNEY BACK TO MY INDIGENOUS ROOTS BY ZAKIYA HAHTA NASHOBA

NATURAL AND ABORIGINAL HISTORY OF TENNESSEE.

CHAPTER I.

The History of Tennessee will be the more perfectly understood, if preceded by a brief statement of the general face of the country, and of its natural productions. This subject, of course sub-divides itself; and requires a description—First, of the general appearance of the country: Secondly, of its marbles, buhr stones and plaister of Paris: Thirdly, of its salt waters: Fourthly, of its petrifactions, ores, volcanic formations, and poisonous tracts. Its geological phenomena may be included in a seperate article; which may be followed by another seperate article, exhibiting the vestiges, of the aboriginal men of America: and this again, by a view of the present races of Indians, who very probably exterminated the aborigines. We shall then come to the settlement of the country by the white people, who at present occupy it, and to the great exertions made by the Indians, to prevent or defeat those settlements.

First, of the general appearance of the country: East Tennessee is divided from North Carolina, by the Unaca or White Mountains—Unica, in the Cherokee language signifying white. The direction of the Mountain is southwest, bearing more to the westward, than the other ridges of the Alleghanies. East of this, is another ridge, the course of

A JOURNEY BACK TO MY INDIGENOUS ROOTS BY ZAKIYA HAHTA NASHOBA

A JOURNEY BACK TO MY INDIGENOUS ROOTS BY ZAKIYA HAHTA NASHOBA

Albert Perry, an "African American" from South Carolina (born circa 1819–1827) his Y chromosome is estimated at 338 thousand years ago

Excerpt from a report

The extremely ancient age combined with the rarity of the A00 lineage, which we also find at very low frequency in central Africa, point to the importance of considering more complex models for the origin of Y chromosome diversity.

These models include ancient population structure and the possibility of archaic introgression of Y chromosomes into anatomically modern humans. The A00 lineage was discovered in a large database of consumer samples of African Americans and has not been identified in traditional hunter-gatherer populations from sub-Saharan Africa.

A JOURNEY BACK TO MY INDIGENOUS ROOTS BY ZAKIYA HAHTA NASHOBA

A JOURNEY BACK TO MY INDIGENOUS ROOTS BY ZAKIYA HAHTA NASHOBA

Reconstruction of earliest bones found in Texas by Prof. Denis Lee

A JOURNEY BACK TO MY INDIGENOUS ROOTS BY ZAKIYA HAHTA NASHOBA

Now let's have a look at Luzia found in Brazil she is but one of over 20 skeletons found classified as the Lagoa Santo race.

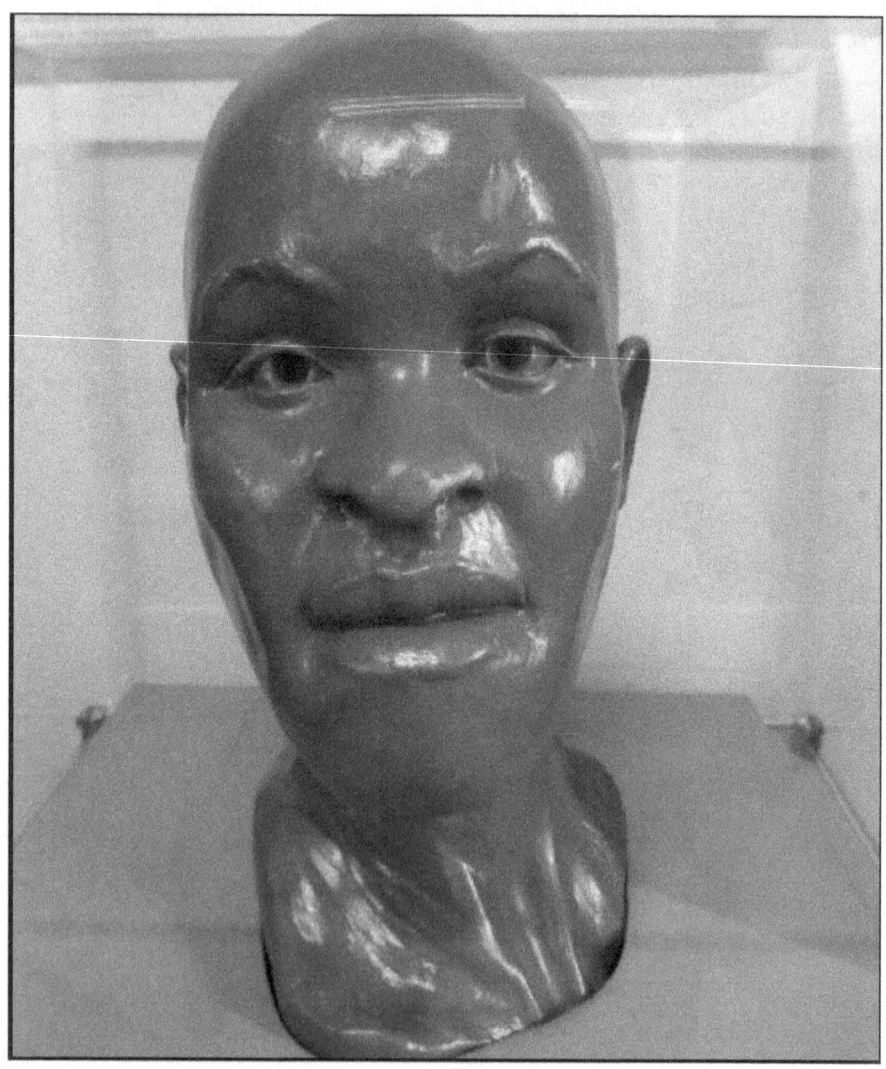

A JOURNEY BACK TO MY INDIGENOUS ROOTS BY ZAKIYA HAHTA NASHOBA

LUZIA. File photo taken on September 20, 1999 of a cameraman recording the presentation of the reconstruction of the head of 'Luzia,' 'the first Brazilian woman' – whose skull is 12,000 years old – at the National Museum of History in Rio de Janeiro, Brazil. File photo by Antonio Scorza/AFP

A JOURNEY BACK TO MY INDIGENOUS ROOTS BY ZAKIYA HAHTA NASHOBA

Now let's take a look at the Ancients of Polynesia called the Lapita culture.

Let me quote an article I found

In 2002, hard new evidence was revealed to the world about the existence of Lapita people, provided by the University of the South Pacific and the Fiji Museum; they unveiled the face of a Lapita woman, who scientists baptized as "Mana" — which means "True." It was reconstructed over a model made of her cranium, found alongside its skeleton at an old human settlement in Naitabale, south of the Moturiki Island, in Central Fiji. This fossil was the subject of scrupulous analysis in Tokyo, Japan; results confirmed it was a person from the Lapita era (1350 to 650 BC). From 2003, Mana's remains rest in Naitabale, Fiji once again.

A JOURNEY BACK TO MY INDIGENOUS ROOTS BY ZAKIYA HAHTA NASHOBA

Here she is Mana of the Lapita Culture

A JOURNEY BACK TO MY INDIGENOUS ROOTS BY ZAKIYA HAHTA NASHOBA

This is a reconstruction of a man found in what is now called Morocco who remains are 160,000 years old, Moesgaard Museum, Denmark.

A JOURNEY BACK TO MY INDIGENOUS ROOTS BY ZAKIYA HAHTA NASHOBA

Now let's take a look at the oldest bones found in Europe called Kostenki 14

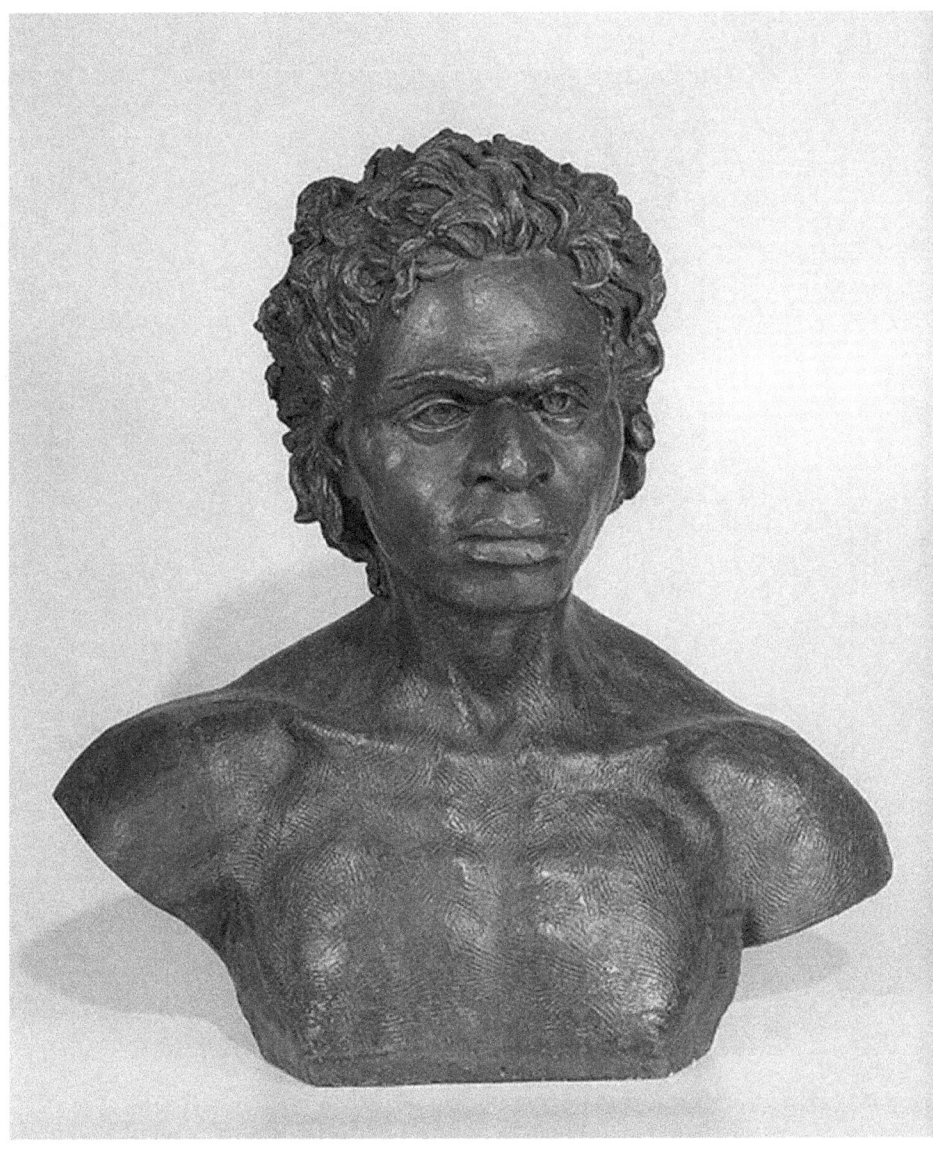

A JOURNEY BACK TO MY INDIGENOUS ROOTS BY ZAKIYA HAHTA NASHOBA

The remains of "Naia," the human skeleton found off the coast of the Yucatan Peninsula of Mexico

A JOURNEY BACK TO MY INDIGENOUS ROOTS BY ZAKIYA HAHTA NASHOBA

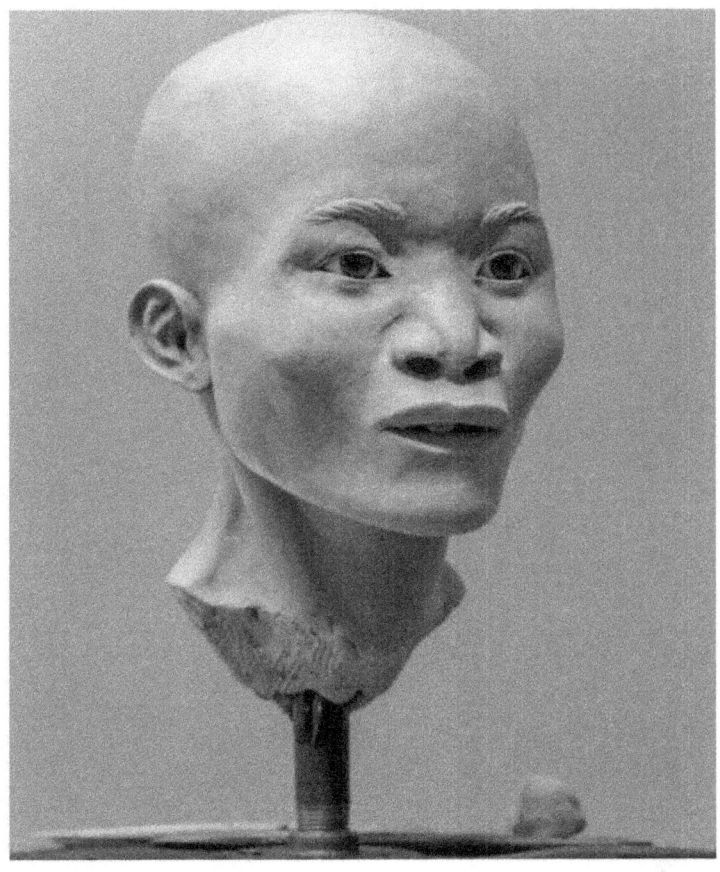

A JOURNEY BACK TO MY INDIGENOUS ROOTS BY ZAKIYA HAHTA NASHOBA

Naia and her modern-day descendant

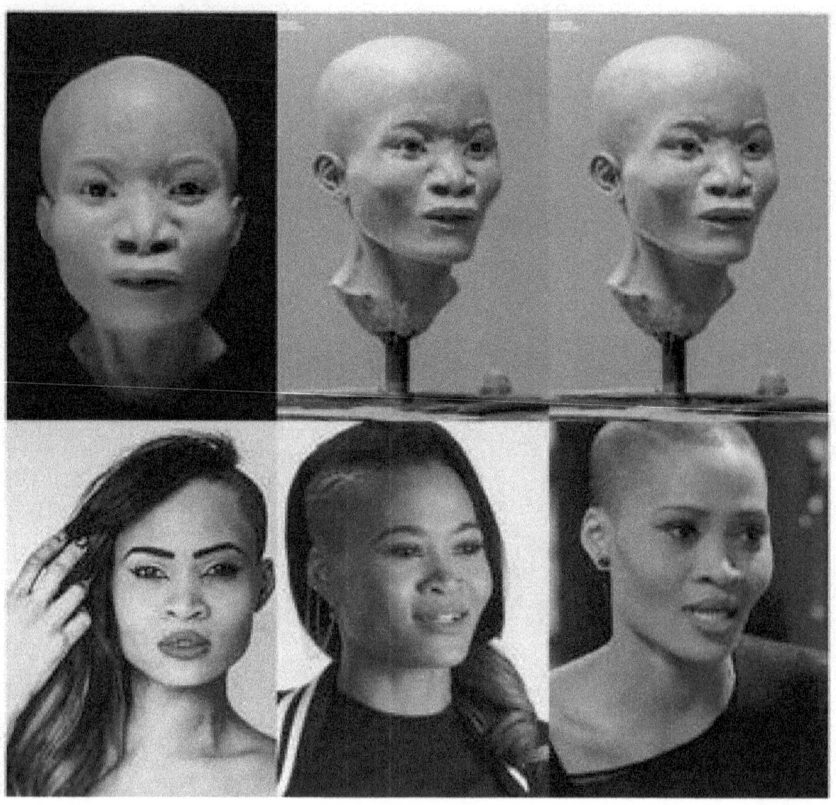

A JOURNEY BACK TO MY INDIGENOUS ROOTS BY ZAKIYA HAHTA NASHOBA

Let me quote an article I found

Archaeologists discovered the skull of Apiuna man about 50 years ago in a cave in Brazil.

Examination of the skull revealed that the prehistoric man resembled Luzia, a name given to an 11,500-year-old skull of a young A woman who is believed to have roamed the savannah of south-central Brazil some 11,500 years ago.

"What was puzzling about Luzia is that her features appeared to be Negroid rather than Mongoloid. This suggests that the Western Hemisphere may have initially been settled not only earlier than thought but by a people distinct from the ancestors of today's North and South American Indians."

A JOURNEY BACK TO MY INDIGENOUS ROOTS BY ZAKIYA HAHTA NASHOBA

Apiuna man

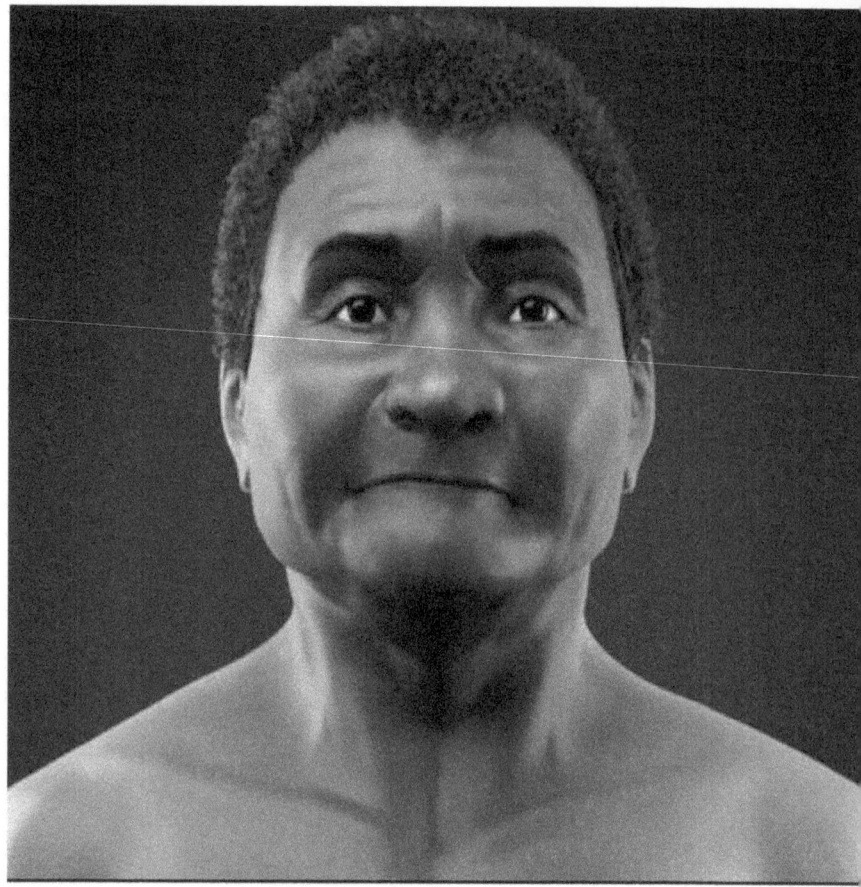

A JOURNEY BACK TO MY INDIGENOUS ROOTS BY ZAKIYA HAHTA NASHOBA

This skeleton, dating back to 1.6 million years, is of a young male *Homo erectus* (KNM-WT 15000; replica) that may have been as young as 8 years of age. Popularly known as "Turkana Boy," it was discovered in 1984 at Nariokotome, west of Lake Turkana, Kenya, by Kamoya Kimeu.

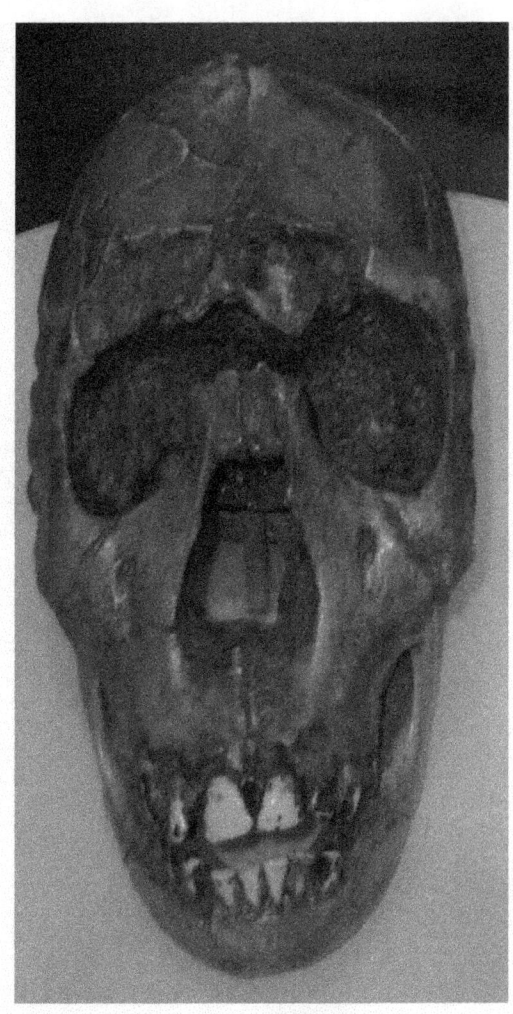

Homo ergaster skull reconstruction of the Turkana Boy/Nariokotome Boy from Lake Turkana, Kenya. Museum of Man, San Diego.

A JOURNEY BACK TO MY INDIGENOUS ROOTS BY ZAKIYA HAHTA NASHOBA

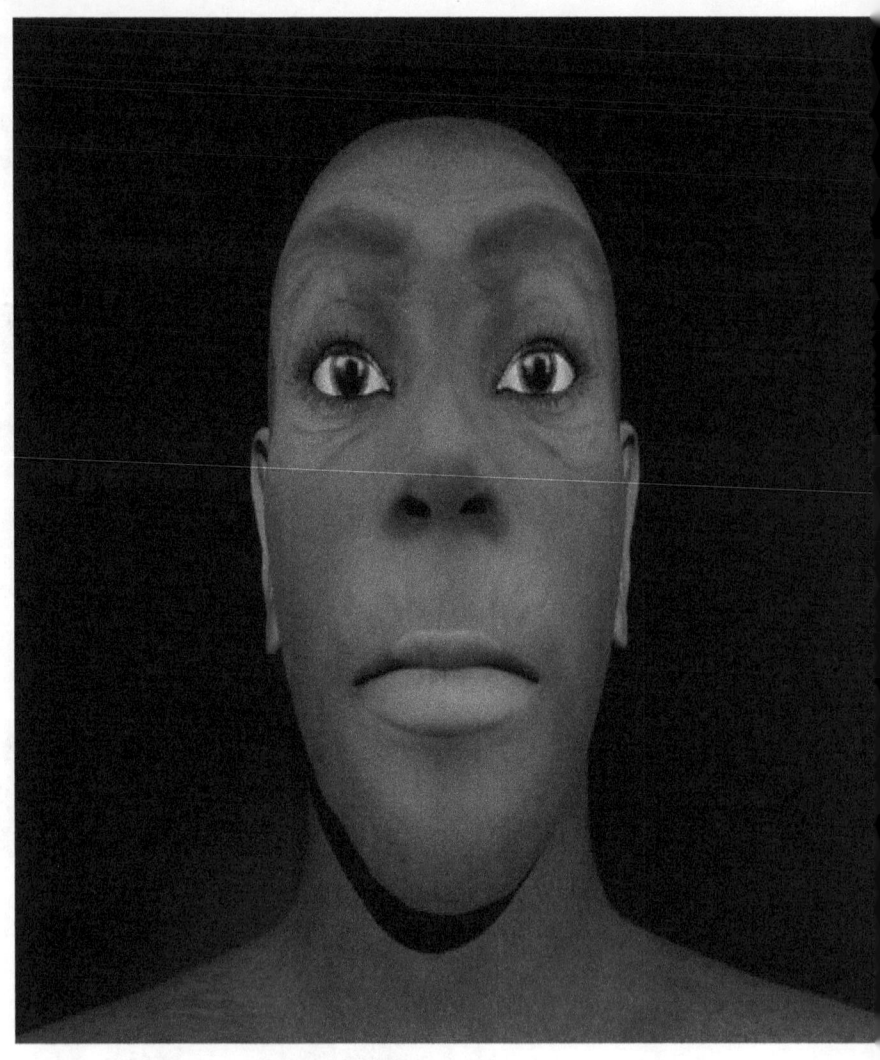

A JOURNEY BACK TO MY INDIGENOUS ROOTS BY ZAKIYA HAHTA NASHOBA

Dubbed the world's oldest child he was found in Smuggler's cave, in Temara, Morocco by Archeologist Harold Dribble

Using the quartz in the soil, the researchers found that the skull is between 108,000 and 110,000 years old, from the same era in which modern human culture emerged.

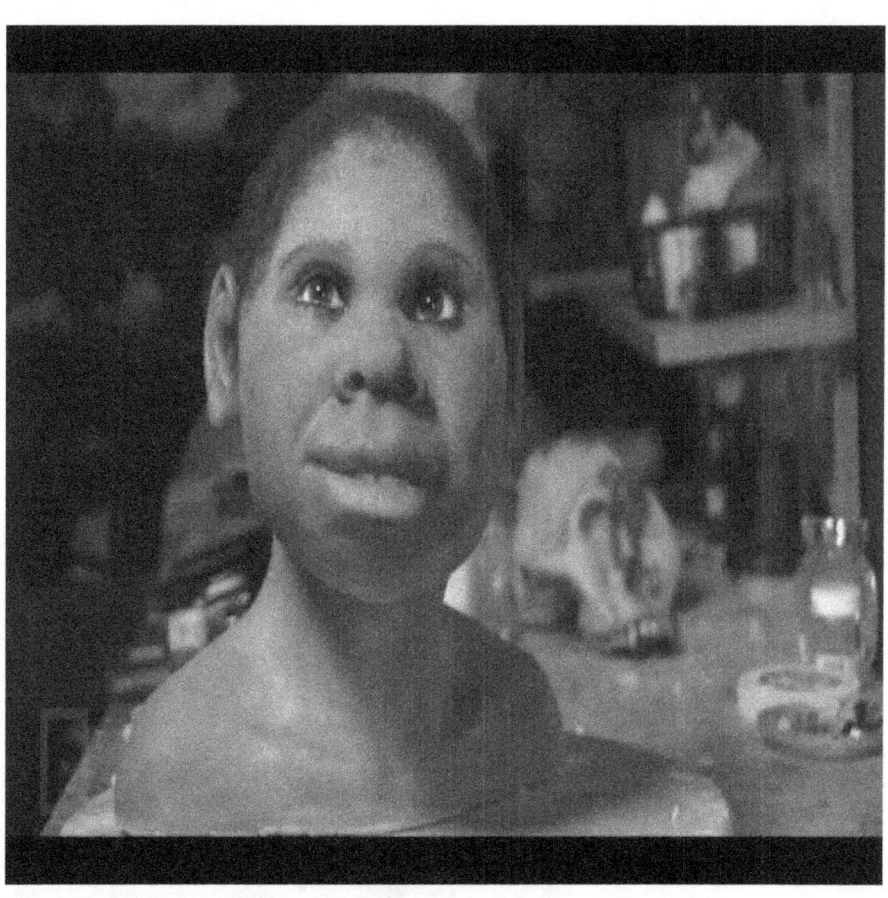

A JOURNEY BACK TO MY INDIGENOUS ROOTS BY ZAKIYA HAHTA NASHOBA

Let me quote an article written by Heather Pringle of National Geographic written in 2017

"At a remote site overlooking the Salish Sea in British Columbia, archaeologists made the discovery of a lifetime in 2010. While digging an ancient shell midden, researchers from the University of Toronto and the local shíshálh Nation were astonished to find the grave of an ancient chief laid to rest nearly 3,700 years ago in a ceremonial bead garment weighing more than 70 pounds" PHOTOGRAPH BY PHILIPPE FROESCH, VISUAL FORENSIC

A JOURNEY BACK TO MY INDIGENOUS ROOTS BY ZAKIYA HAHTA NASHOBA

Chumash artifacts in Santa Barbara museum

A JOURNEY BACK TO MY INDIGENOUS ROOTS BY ZAKIYA HAHTA NASHOBA

Ancient Pre - Columbian Moche culture in Peru from 100 to 700 AD

A JOURNEY BACK TO MY INDIGENOUS ROOTS BY ZAKIYA HAHTA NASHOBA

Pre - Columbian figure this one reminds me of the singer Ciara

A JOURNEY BACK TO MY INDIGENOUS ROOTS BY ZAKIYA HAHTA NASHOBA

Pre – Colombian figure this one reminds me of Master P

A JOURNEY BACK TO MY INDIGENOUS ROOTS BY ZAKIYA HAHTA NASHOBA

Pre – Colombian Mayan Stela in Copan Honduras this one reminds me of my brother I have been to this site.

A JOURNEY BACK TO MY INDIGENOUS ROOTS BY ZAKIYA HAHTA NASHOBA

Mayan before the Spanish (European) amalgamation

A JOURNEY BACK TO MY INDIGENOUS ROOTS BY ZAKIYA HAHTA NASHOBA

Figure 3: Zemi, front and back views, ca. 1510-15. Museo Nazionale Preistorico ed Etnografico "Luigi Pigorini," Rome, Italy

This zemi (Deity) is one of the most elaborate of the works created by Taíno craftsmen on the cusp of the 16th century.

Taino is an umbrella term for the indigenous people of the Caribbean Greater Antilles

A JOURNEY BACK TO MY INDIGENOUS ROOTS BY ZAKIYA HAHTA NASHOBA

A JOURNEY BACK TO MY INDIGENOUS ROOTS BY ZAKIYA HAHTA NASHOBA

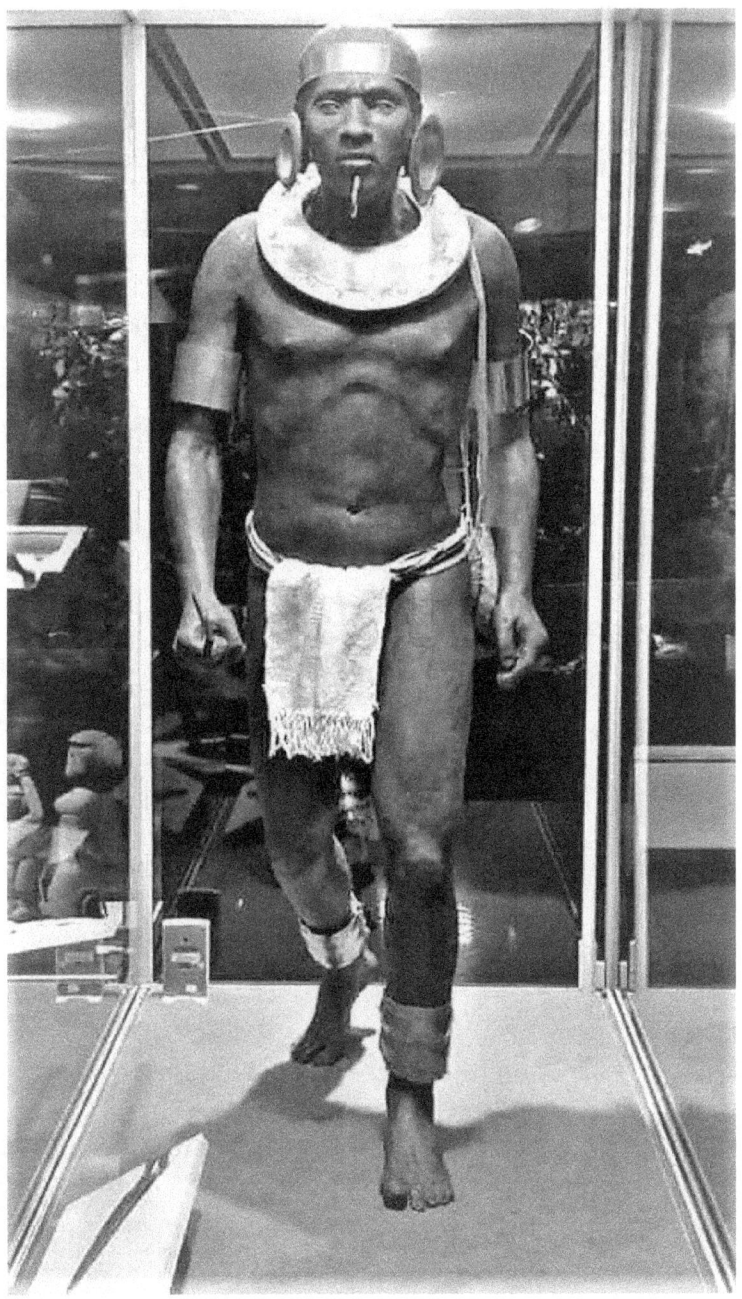

Central America

A JOURNEY BACK TO MY INDIGENOUS ROOTS BY ZAKIYA HAHTA NASHOBA

A JOURNEY BACK TO MY INDIGENOUS ROOTS BY ZAKIYA HAHTA NASHOBA

THE ST. LOUIS MEDICAL REVIEW

A Monthly Journal of Medicine, Surgery, and the Allied Sciences

Volume LX   DECEMBER, 1911   Number 12

MAN AS A GEOLOGIC SPECIES IN THE WESTERN HEMISPHERE.

By ALBERT S. ASHMEAD, M. D.,

New York.

PART V.

Was primitive man in America a negro? The answer to this question leans to the affirmative.

The dense shadow of the centuries covers the primitive history of America with an impenetrable veil which, probably, science can never raise. What is the origin of American man? This is a problem which, since the first epochs of the discovery of the New World, has most highly interested men of science and thinkers in general. Hundreds of volumes have been written about hypotheses, more or less ingenious, whose systems, as erudite as chaquian of the eastern Andean regions of Argentina and Patagonian pampas, where most ancient reptilian mammoth fossils have been found, there is not known anything of the architecture, and merely a few remains, isolated vestiges of the mysterious civilization, of those unknown people on the coasts of Ecuador, and in the Valley of San Augustine, Colombia, were worked gigantic statues of stone idols, impossible gods, unrelated to any later cultured state of man; for instance, that of the monoliths of the Tiahuanaico ruins, which are pre-Incasic. There huge statues of

A JOURNEY BACK TO MY INDIGENOUS ROOTS BY ZAKIYA HAHTA NASHOBA

ed in the more peaceful grassy plains with the horses. These last man had learned, in Ancient France, to use as foodstuff. The culture states of man changed, in accordance with physical requirement, everywhere differently.

The primitive zone of dispersion of these Pampeans is recognizable readily by the word a frozen planet, for thousands of years.

There were many tribes of Indians at the time of the discovery of the Western hemisphere, who are thought by scientists to belong to a negro race. Such were the Otomies of Mexico, the Caracoles of Haiti, the Argahos of Cutara, the Aravos of Orinoco, the

December, 1911.   THE ST. LOUIS MEDICAL REVIEW.   357

Matayas of Brazil, the Manabis of Quito, the Chuanas of Darien.

Gomars (*Hist. General de India*) speaks of negro slaves who were held on Panama soil. The negroes figure with frequency in most remote traditions of Peru, and of other American peoples. These men were "little and black" and "lived in groves and woods." Certain tribes (Ernesto Restreps, *au Viaji all Darien*) attribute the origin of their nation to an Indian with two wives, one a negress, who lived on the shores of Tatarcuna. To this race is referred some ancient skeletons, of peculiar structure, very distinct from those of the red American race.

Worthy of attention are two crania of exaggerated prognathesis, with retreating foreheads, and apophyses very well unfolded, the feature of negroid type. The same thing is seen in ancient Mexican sculpture related to a period anterior to that of the Otomies, such as the great diocritic head of Huayepan and the giant hatchet of Vera Cruz, whose head presents a great similarity with the figure of the woman of the statue of San Augustine. Both have identical features, and are of a same style, and obedient to the same model, that of the antochthonous negro race, whose dispersed remains were encountered by the conquerors, and upon which was founded later, the so-called American red race.

New facts and discoveries will doubtless confirm this supposition, that the primitive American population was a negroid race. We know only, today, the culture states of about three groups of most ancient man in Amer-

A JOURNEY BACK TO MY INDIGENOUS ROOTS BY ZAKIYA HAHTA NASHOBA

Are you starting to realize just how much they have lied to us about who the indigenous population of the world is?

This makes it a little bit harder to witness these ancient descendants get slaughtered in the streets because they are now labeled Black and African American, meanwhile the media continuously shows the systematic slaughtering of Indigenous peoples, now revisit Jim Crow for a moment and put it in the perspective of indigenous peoples being enslaved, beaten, raped and eaten, yes I said eaten by European Immigrants the skins was boiled down to make oil and some skin was made into furniture, purses, wallets etc. nowadays it's done through mass organ harvesting via abortions and deaths.

There were no such places named America or Africa 1,000 years ago neither was the theory of a continental drift the Earth was populated simultaneously and all its inhabitants were of a dark hue ranging in various shades of brown from the lightest brown to the darkest now known as black.

Rise sleeping giants and sleep no more you are the Ancient Ones.

A JOURNEY BACK TO MY INDIGENOUS ROOTS BY ZAKIYA HAHTA NASHOBA

Paper genocide

In my research I found three of my families surname on Walter Ashby Plecker hit list these surnames are

Locklear (my maternal line)

Johnson and Robinson

(My paternal line from Kentucky which used to be Virginia)

My Great Grandparents x2 was held against their will and labeled slaves this happened in Kentucky they were mentioned in the book clasping hands with generations past by Emma Rouse Lloyd

My Great Grandparents are John Robinson, Peggy Smith, Andrew Robinson, Catherine Sechrets, Moss Sechrets and Marsalla Sechrets.

A JOURNEY BACK TO MY INDIGENOUS ROOTS BY ZAKIYA HAHTA NASHOBA

I will include an excerpt but before that read this

Br'er Rabbit at the Square Ground

Pennsylvania Journal in 1747 advertised for a runaway, "a very lusty Negro fellow named Sampson," who had an Indian mother, looked like an Indian, talked and dressed like an Indian, as did his son, and presumably was fleeing to Indian relatives in Carolina.[16] Frank Freeman, a former North Carolina slave, recounted how his father, who had Indian blood, "passed for a free nigger."[17] On the eve of the Revolution a fugitive slave notice appeared in the *Virginia Gazette* for Phebe, a remarkable white Indian woman who, dressed like a Negro, had run off with a mulatto.[18] Upon occasion in colonial times one might see references to "a Negro man of the Indian breed" or a "mustee [mestizo] Negro fellow."

At an early period an undetermined number of full-blooded or mixed-blood Indians were characterized as Negroes. The names of Negro slaves occasionally afford a clue as to their ethnic background, yet at times one is left more confused than ever. Except that Indians normally cost less, masters made little distinction between African and Indian slaves. All were indiscriminately thrown together in the quarters, sent out to the fields, and employed as artisans and domestics. Slaves were given Christian names, which, at least in the white man's world, were the only

A JOURNEY BACK TO MY INDIGENOUS ROOTS BY ZAKIYA HAHTA NASHOBA

Let's take a look at the laws established by the European immigrant's source is The American Journal of Sociology, Volume 21 the article mentions Kanaka that's Hawaiian, the Indian, Negro, Chinese, and Kanaka mentioned below are all of Negro stock thus the prohibition of marrying European immigrants aka white women.

Then you can read about my great Grandparent's x3 John Robinson and Peggy Smith and my great grandparents X2 Andrew Robinson and Catherine (Kate) Sechrets it hurt for me to read this about my grandparents and just how nonchalantly people can talk about enslaving another human being.

Moss and Marsalla are Catherine's parents Marsalla ran away once her kidnapper died and willed her to another man, she refused to continue living life enslaved the family doesn't know what became of her.

So far these are the only grandparents I have found that were enslaved and that's because there was a paper trail.

A JOURNEY BACK TO MY INDIGENOUS ROOTS BY ZAKIYA HAHTA NASHOBA

dollars, or be imprisoned in the county jail not less than six months or more than one year, or both."

North Carolina (Revised Code, 1905).

Vol. I, sec. 2083: "All marriages between a white person and a negro or Indian, or between a white person and a person of negro or Indian descent to the third generation, inclusive, shall be void."

North Dakota (Compiled Laws, 1913).

Chap. 31, Miscegenation. Sec. 9582: Marriage between white and negro persons: "It shall be unlawful for any white male person, residing or being in this State, to intermarry with any negro female person; and it shall be in like manner unlawful for any white female person, residing or being in this State, to intermarry with any negro male person, and every marriage hereafter formed and solemnized in contravention of the provisions of this section shall be utterly null and void and either or both of the contracting parties to such surreptitious marriage shall be punished by imprisonment in the State penitentiary for a term not exceeding ten years or by a fine not exceeding two thousand dollars or by both fine and imprisonment."

Sec. 9583. "Definition of a negro person: Every person who shall have one-eighth or more negro blood shall be deemed and held to be a colored person or negro."

Oklahoma (Revised Laws, 1910).

Sec. 3894: "The marriage of any person of African descent, as defined by the constitution of this State,[1] to any person not of African descent, or the marriage of any person not of African descent to any person of African descent, shall be unlawful and is hereby prohibited within this State."

Oregon (Bellinger and Cotton Code, 1902).

Sec. 5217: "What marriages are void: 3. When either of the parties is a white person and the other negro, or Mongolian or a person of one-fourth or more of negro or Mongolian blood."

Sec. 1999: "Hereafter it shall not be lawful within this state for any white person, male or female, to intermarry with any negro, Chinese, or any person having one-fourth or more negro, Chinese or Kanaka blood, or any person having more than one-half Indian blood, ... and all such marriages, or attempted marriages, shall be absolutely null and void."

South Carolina (Civil Code, 1902).

Sec. 2664: "It shall be unlawful for any white man to intermarry with any woman of either the Indian or negro races, or any mulatto, mestizo or half-breed, ... or for any white woman to intermarry with any person other than a white man, or for any mulatto, half-breed, Indian, negro, or mestizo to intermarry with a white woman; and any such marriage, or attempted marriage, shall be utterly null and void and of no effect."[2]

South Dakota (Compiled Laws, 1913).

Chap. 266, Laws of 1913. Sec. 1: "The intermarriage or illicit cohabitation of any persons belonging to the African, Corean, Malayan or Mongolian race, with any person of the opposite sex, belonging to the Caucasian or white race, is hereby prohibited, and any person who shall hereafter enter into any such marriage, or who shall indulge in any such illicit cohabitation shall be deemed guilty of a felony and upon conviction thereof shall be punished by a fine of not exceeding one thousand dollars or by imprisonment in the State prison for a term not exceeding ten years or both such fine and imprisonment."

Tennessee (Code, 1896).

Sec. 4186: "The intermarriage of white persons with negroes, mulattoes, or persons of mixed blood descended from a negro, to the third generation inclusive, or their living together as man and wife in this state, is hereby prohibited."

Texas (Willson's Criminal Statutes, 1906).

Art. 346: Intermarriage of whites and blacks: "If any white person and negro shall knowingly intermarry with each other within this state, or, having so intermarried, in or out of the state, shall continue to live together as man and wife within this state, they shall be punished by confinement in the penitentiary for a term not less than two or more than five years."

Art. 347: "Negro" and "White person" defined: "The term 'negro,' as used in the preceding article, includes also a person of mixed blood descended from negro ancestry to the third generation inclusive, although one ancestor of each generation may have been a white person. All persons not included in the definition of 'negro' shall be deemed a white person within the meaning of this article."

Utah (Revised Statutes, 1898).

Sec. 1184: "Marriage is prohibited and declared void: between a negro and a white person," and "between a Mongolian and a white person."

Virginia (Pollard's Code, 1904).

Sec. 2252: "What marriages are void: All marriages between a white person and a colored person, ... shall be absolutely void, without any decree of divorce or other legal process."

Note. "A marriage between a white man and a woman who is less than one-fourth negro blood, however small the lesser quantity may be, is legal."

West Virginia (Code of 1906).

Sec. 2917: "Void marriages: 1. All marriages between a white person and a negro."

A JOURNEY BACK TO MY INDIGENOUS ROOTS BY ZAKIYA HAHTA NASHOBA

OUR COLORED FOLK

THIS record should not be closed without speaking briefly of the colored branch of the family—the slaves. In our own family we had but two slaves, Jack, a finely built, ebony black young fellow whom my father heired from his family, and Mary, a middle-aged woman, half Indian, who did the cooking, cleaning, milking, etc.

My grandmother Henderson owned three families:

John Robinson and *Peggy* (Smith) were married by a white minister before my grandfather owned them. Their children were—Lewis, George, Aaron, Andrew, Julius and Liza.

Lewis, after the negroes were freed, went to St. Louis and was coachman for one family for twenty-nine years.

George and *Aaron* died in infancy.

Andrew married *Kate,* daughter of "Moss" Sechrist, owned by Charles Sechrist. They had eighteen children. Andrew died in the summer of 1931, aged ninety-two years. Kate died several years previous. Grandmother did not own Kate.

Julius was a stupid young fellow, of not much account. After the war he lived on the Whitney Wilson place on the Independence Pike.

Liza married and was living in Williamstown when we last heard of her. She had two children. She lived with the Rouse family for a few years as nurse for Henderson and John T. The Robinson family lived in a log cabin in the lot north of the "big house."

A JOURNEY BACK TO MY INDIGENOUS ROOTS BY ZAKIYA HAHTA NASHOBA

After they were freed, *John* and *Peggy* lived on the Nath Thompson place and later went near Richwood. After John died Peggy lived with Andrew's family. She and John are buried in the family burying

CLASPING HANDS WITH GENERATIONS PAST

ground on Andrew's farm near Richwood. Andrew was a good citizen and a prosperous farmer. He owned his own home and farm where one of his sons now lives. Grandfather bought this family of six from Robert Daniels.

Patience had six children: "Whit" whose father was an Indian, Harve, Parthene, Ruth, Milly (Pig) and Jim.

Parthene was maid in "Miss Lizzie's" family. Ruth was "Miss Hannah's" maid and Milly known as "Pig" lived with "Miss Nan" and was nurse for the first baby in the family. When the writer was about ten years old the family lived in Crittenden. Early one morning there was a great commotion in the kitchen and child-like, she ran out to see what was going on. When she opened the kitchen door a great big, very black, thick-lipped woman snatched her up and holding her close to her breast smothered her with kisses, exclaiming, "O, my precious baby!" It was "Pig" who was passing through the village and ran in to see "her baby" while the stage horses were being changed. At that time Milly (Pig) was a hair dresser in Lexington. Whit lived with her and assisted in her business.

Letty had two children, Lee and Dick (Williams).

**Dan's* wife belonged to the Collins family and lived with them. Dan and Whit got into some trouble and Grandma sent them to Tennessee. Whit returned after the war but Dan never came back though he often wrote to Grandma.

Peggy cooked in the brick kitchen before an open fire for the "big house." Letty cooked for the slaves in the frame cabin which stood in

A JOURNEY BACK TO MY INDIGENOUS ROOTS BY ZAKIYA HAHTA NASHOBA

As soon as my Father told me about our family cemetery, I immediately went to work restoring the true identity of my ancestors whose bones lay there.

I reached out to the historical society in Kentucky and began to tell them my family history I submitted some documents to them because they wanted to do an article in the library newspaper about my family and I.

I asked them who would I have to speak to in order to correct the atrocity of labeling my families burial ground as a "Negro" cemetery? I was then directed to contact the Boone County Historic Preservation Review Board in Kentucky

I reached out to an employee there who had informed me that someone had already called about me he sent me a form to update my family information and he designated the site as a Native American burial site he said that the site could never be disturbed and no bones could ever be removed for any reason, my family burial site is a small family cemetery it is unregulated by Kentucky

I will be purchasing a monument to be placed at the site to notify not only the neighbors but anyone who see the site that it is a burial site of Indigenous Americans.

A JOURNEY BACK TO MY INDIGENOUS ROOTS BY ZAKIYA HAHTA NASHOBA

Now I see just how my family was directly affected by racism and paper genocide, it is important to note that even if a surname is not listed it doesn't mean people have not suffered paper genocide this letter happens to be something practiced in all the colony's we are just fortunate enough to be able to see these PRIVATE communications.

(He never intended for us to see them)

A JOURNEY BACK TO MY INDIGENOUS ROOTS BY ZAKIYA HAHTA NASHOBA

18 years earlier in 1925, he wrote yet another racist letter that mentioned my Robinson surname

COMMONWEALTH OF VIRGINIA
BUREAU OF VITAL STATISTICS
STATE BOARD OF HEALTH
RICHMOND

ENNION G. WILLIAMS, M. D., COMMISSIONER
W. A. PLECKER, M. D., REGISTRAR OF VITAL STATISTICS

May 9, 1925.

Hon. A. T. Shields,
Rockbridge County Clerk's Office,
Lexington, Virginia.

Dear Sir:

In reply to your letter of May 4th, which came during my absence from the office, I beg to advise that the matter in reference to an appeal in the Atha Sorrells case was left to the Attorney General and the lawyer, Mr. Shewmake, employed by the Anglo Saxon Clubs. After going over carefully the evidence, in view of the fact that nothing new could be introduced, they decided that it was unwise to appeal the case as the only evidence upon which we absolutely relied, that of our records was set aside by Judge Holt, and we would not care to take the risk of having the Supreme Court render a similar decision. Our hope is to drift along until the next legislature, and have them pass a bill preventing the marriage of the Indians with the whites. In my judgement there are no native Indians in Virginia unmixed with negro blood.

As to the Robinson, Hartless, and Tyree people, I think if you will get their pedigree, and trace it up in their old birth records, you will be pretty apt to find that part of them, if not all of them, will be recorded as colored. In more recent years, however, especially since the decision in 1876, a considerable proportion of them, just as in the cases you mentioned, have been married as white. I do not know how you can avoid it, as we would not care to have another case tested in Court. It would really be better if they would accept it, to enter them as Indians, and we can have the whole Indian outfit handled at one time by the legislature. They seem to be satisfied to be called Indian.

I am telling you this, however, as a matter of confidence, as we would not care to arouse opposition in advance. It looks now very much as if a considerable portion of the Rockbridge tribe has gotten away from us, and that we will find it a hard matter to properly classify them in the future. Judge Holt's unfortunate decision has greatly emboldened them. In Amherst County, however, we are still able to hold them in place.

I would suggest that you confer with our Mr. V. W. Davis, of Fairfield, who seems familiar with the facts. He wrote us a letter which might be considered confidential, and I would not care to quote from it, but you can talk to him yourself.

Very truly yours,

STATE REGISTRAR.

WAP/P

A JOURNEY BACK TO MY INDIGENOUS ROOTS BY ZAKIYA HAHTA NASHOBA

has special file
Dr. Plecker

COMMONWEALTH OF VIRGINIA
Department of Health
Bureau of Vital Statistics
Richmond

January 1943.

Local Registrars, Physicians, Health
Officers, Nurses, School Superintendents,
and Clerks of the Courts

Dear Co-workers:

Our December 1942 letter to local registrars, also mailed to the clerks, set forth the determined effort to escape from the negro race of groups of "free issues," or descendants of the "free mulattoes" of early days, so listed prior to 1865 in the United States census and various types of State records, as distinguished from slave negroes.

Now that these people are playing up the advantages gained by being permitted to give "Indian" as the race of the child's parents on birth certificates, we see the great mistake made in not stopping earlier the organized propagation of this racial falsehood. They have been using the advantage thus gained as an aid to intermarriage into the white race and to attend white schools, and now for some time they have been refusing to register with war draft boards as negroes, as required by the boards which are faithfully performing their duties. Three of these negroes from Caroline County were sentenced to prison on January 12 in the United States Court at Richmond for refusing to obey the draft law unless permitted to classify themselves as "Indians."

Some of these mongrels, finding that they have been able to sneak in their birth certificates unchallenged as Indians are now making a rush to register as white. Upon investigation we find that a few local registrars have been permitting such certificates to pass through their hands unquestioned and without warning our office of the fraud. Those attempting this fraud should be warned that they are liable to a penalty of one year in the penitentiary (Section 5099a of the Code). Several clerks have likewise been actually granting them licenses to marry whites, or at least to marry amongst themselves as Indian or white. The danger of this error always confronts the clerk who does not inquire carefully as to the residence of the woman when he does not have positive information. The law is explicit that the license be issued by the clerk of the county or city in which the woman resides.

To aid all of you in determining just which are the mixed families, we have made a list of their surnames by counties and cities, as complete as possible at this time. This list should be preserved by all, even by those in counties and cities not included, as these people are moving around over the State and changing race at the new place. A family has just been investigated which was always recorded as negro around Glade Springs, Washington County, but which changed to white and married as such in Roanoke County. This is going on constantly and can be prevented only by care on the part of local registrars, clerks, doctors, health workers, and school authorities.

Please report all known or suspicious cases to the Bureau of Vital Statistics, giving names, ages, parents, and as much other information as possible. All certificates of these people showing "Indian" or "white" are now being rejected and returned to the physician or midwife, but local registrars hereafter must not permit them to pass their hands uncorrected or unchallenged and without a note of warning to us. One hundred and fifty thousand other mulattoes in Virginia are watching eagerly the attempt of their pseudo-Indian brethren, ready to follow in a rush when the first have made a break in the dike.

Very truly yours,

W. A. Plecker, M. D.
State Registrar of Vital Statistics

A JOURNEY BACK TO MY INDIGENOUS ROOTS BY ZAKIYA HAHTA NASHOBA

Ramsey Branham no white Branham in Amherst Co— Dr. Plecker 3-14-46

SURNAMES, BY COUNTIES AND CITIES, OF MIXED NEGROID VIRGINIA FAMILIES STRIVING TO PASS AS "INDIAN" OR WHITE.

Albemarle:	Moon, Powell, Kidd, Pumphrey.
Amherst: (Migrants to Alleghany and Campbell)	Adcock (Adcox), Beverly (this family is now trying to evade the situation by adopting the name of Burch or Birch, which was the name of the white mother of the present adult generation), Branham, Duff, Floyd, Hamilton, Hartless, Hicks, Johns, Lawless, Nuckles (Knuckles), Painter, Ramsey, Redcross, Roberts, Southards (Suthards, Southerds, Southers), Sorrells, Terry, Tyree, Willis, Clark, Cash, Wood.
Bedford:	McVey, Maxey, Branham, Burley. (See Amherst County)
Rockbridge: (Migrants to Augusta)	Cash, Clark, Coleman, Duff, Floyd, Hartless, Hicks, Mason, Mayse (Mays), Painters, Pultz, Ramsey, Southerds (Southers, Southards, Suthards), Sorrells, Terry, Tyree, Wood, Johns.
Charles City:	Collins, Dennis, Bradby, Howell, Langston, Stewart, Wynn, Adkins.
King William:	Collins, Dennis, Bradby, Howell, Langston, Stewart, Wynn, Custalow (Custaloe), Dungee, Holmes, Miles, Page, Allmond, Adams, Hawkes, Spurlock, Doggett.
New Kent:	Collins, Bradby, Stewart, Wynn, Adkins, Langston.
Henrico and Richmond City:	See Charles City, New Kent, and King William.
Caroline:	Byrd, Fortune, Nelson. (See Essex)
Essex and King and Queen:	Nelson, Fortune, Byrd, Cooper, Tate, Hammond, Brooks, Boughton, Prince, Mitchell, Robinson.
Elizabeth City & Newport News:	Stewart (descendants of Charles City families).
Halifax:	Epps (Eppes), Stewart (Stuart), Coleman, Johnson, Martin, Talley, Sheppard (Shepard), Young.
Norfolk County & Portsmouth:	Sawyer, Bass, Weaver, Locklear (Locklair), King, Bright, Porter, Ingram.
Westmoreland:	Sorrells, Worlds (or Worrell), Atwells, Gutridge, Oliff.
Greene:	Shifflett, Shiflet.
Prince William:	Tyson, Segar. (See Fauquier)
Fauquier:	Hoffman (Huffman), Riley, Colvin, Phillips. (See Prince William)
Lancaster:	Dorsey (Dawson).
Washington:	Beverly, Barlow, Thomas, Hughes, Lethcoe, Worley.
Roanoke County:	Beverly. (See Washington)
Lee and Smyth:	Collins, Gibson (Gipson), Moore, Goins, Ramsey, Delph, Bunch, Freeman, Mise, Barlow, Bolden (Bolin), Mullins, Hawkins. — Chiefly Tennessee "Melungeons."
Scott:	Dingus. (See Lee County)
Russell:	Keith, Castell, Stillwell, Meade, Proffitt. (See Lee & Tazewell)
Tazewell:	Hammed, Duncan. (See Russell)
Wise:	See Lee, Smyth, Scott, and Russell Counties.

A JOURNEY BACK TO MY INDIGENOUS ROOTS BY ZAKIYA HAHTA NASHOBA

Mr. Turner McDowell,
Clerk of the Circuit Court,
Botetourt County,
Fincastle, Virginia.

Dear Mr. McDowell:

A citizen of Rockbridge County sent us a newspaper clipping reading as follows: "Mr. and Mrs. F. W. Mohler announces the marriage of their daughter, Grace Vernon, to Samuel Christian Branham, of Buchanan, Saturday, September 18, at the Fincastle Methodist parsonage by the Rev. Sites."

Our informant writes as follows:

"This family of Mohlers, living in Lexington, Va., belongs to the class of respectable white people, making about ninety percent of the rural population of the state. These Branhams moved into Rockbridge from Amherst about two years ago. They are unquestionably mixed blood, negroid in every appearance, speech and behavior.

"This man moved just over the line into Botetourt Co., recently for the purpose, I am sure, of obtaining a license at Fincastle, the family history being well known in Lexington, this County. Unless I am mistaken, this is clearly an unlawful marriage in Virginia."

This is a favorite trick of these mixed breeds. They go around to other counties where they are not known and in their applications swear that they are white. These people are usually well known in their own counties and their clerks will not issue licenses for them to marry white people. Did this woman give Lexington, Virginia as her place of residence? If so, Section 5072 specifies that the license shall be issued by the clerk of the Circuit Court of the county or city in which the female usually resides. If this feature of the law were strictly adhered to, many of the mixed marriages would be prevented, as the clerks at the place of residence usually know the facts, while those of the adjoining counties do not.

A JOURNEY BACK TO MY INDIGENOUS ROOTS BY ZAKIYA HAHTA NASHOBA

> According to the law of Virginia, this couple cannot be married. This marriage is null and void. Do you know where they are living now? We have made a thorough study of the racial origin of this Branham family. All of the Amherst County Branhams are classed as "free issue", descendants of the antebellum freed negroes. We are sending a copy of this letter to the Commonwealth's Attorney.
>
> In your reply, please give us the name of all of the parents as they show on the application.
>
> Very truly yours,
> W. A. Plecker, M. D.
> State Registrar.
> WAP:W

A JOURNEY BACK TO MY INDIGENOUS ROOTS BY ZAKIYA HAHTA NASHOBA

Every " Indigenous American" does NOT have straight hair and high cheekbones, every "Indigenous American" does NOT have pale skin, round faces, hook noses or Asian looking eyes, stop acting like these are the only indigenous features found here in America (The Continent).

Every "Indigenous American" is NOT a part of a Federally recognized tribe, so stop acting like that is a what makes indigenous blood legitimate.

Stop acting like we all call ourselves "Native American", "Indian", or "American Indian", those are all colonized terms forced on indigenous people.

Stop using colonization as the standard for indigenous identity...

A JOURNEY BACK TO MY INDIGENOUS ROOTS BY ZAKIYA HAHTA NASHOBA

Acknowledgments

To all my Ancient relations both near and far thank you for being my strength on this journey.

To everyone affected by paper genocide and colonization NEVER GIVE UP you must continue to restore your family legacy, your future generations deserve to know who they are.

To the Indigenous American community whose skin is as deep and dark as the fertile soil thank you for using your platforms to tell the world that we are NOT African we are Indigenous to the entire continent of America, although some of us may have admixtures from many populations none of those admixtures can remove us from our mother soil, the continent of America is our motherland.

A JOURNEY BACK TO MY INDIGENOUS ROOTS BY ZAKIYA HAHTA NASHOBA

A JOURNEY BACK TO MY INDIGENOUS ROOTS BY ZAKIYA HAHTA NASHOBA

About the Author

Zakiya Hahta Nashoba is an indigenous American Historian, Chief of her Tribe, Creator of Indigenous Peoples United and an Indigenous Energy Healer, her greatest accomplishment in life is being a Mother to her two daughters everything else pales in comparison.

In her free time, she enjoys making indigenous jewelry

(beading, jewelry wrapping etc.)

Her website is www.indigenouspeoplesunited.org

Her email is ipu@indigenouspeoplesunited.org

Her YouTube channel is Hahta Nashoba

www.ingramcontent.com/pod-product-compliance
Lightning Source LLC
Chambersburg PA
CBHW031630160426
43196CB00006B/349